The Winter of Life

Redeeming the Time

The Winter of Life

Redeeming the Time

Sewell Hall

The Winter of Life

Published by Mount Bethel Publishing,
P.O. Box 123, Port Murray, NJ 07865,
www.MountBethelPublishing.com

ISBN: 978-0-9850059-5-5

Cover Design: - Bethany Hubartt, Photos - Gardner Hall

Printed in the United States of America

With deep gratitude to members of
the Embry Hills Church
in Atlanta who have supported me
through nearly half of
my years of preaching and have
given me the opportunity
to remain actively involved,
even into the Winter of Life.

Contents

Chapter 1

The Winter of Life

"You have made summer and winter" *(Psalm 74:17).*

Old age has been called the winter of life. Why? Most obviously, I suppose, because of the idea that old age comes at the end of life just as winter comes at the end of the year.

There may be other reasons. Winter is a time when many activities must be curtailed. So it is with old age. Activities that have been very much a part of our usual day are no longer possible.

Then, too, like winter weather, old people are often cold. Have you ever visited an old person in the winter and found the room so hot you could hardly breathe? Young people don't understand, but old people do. Even King David suffered from being cold. I like the King James translation of 1 Kings 1:1. "Now king David was old and stricken in years; and they covered him with clothes, but he gat no heat."

Not All Bad

Winter is not all bad. It is a time for remembering the activities of the past year with pleasure and making plans to do better. In the winter many people write a family letter detailing the year's history.

When the snow is coming down, once we have come to terms with the frustration of not being able to do the things we planned, there is something pleasant about having the time just to sit quietly and meditate.

Winter is a time when families get together, and what a joy it is for old folks when they have the family together. They have longed to see their children and grandchildren, and now they have come to visit for a while.

Even the silence of a snow-covered landscape is pleasant, something like the relief an old man feels as he turns down the hearing aid to gain relief from the noise in the house.

Not All Good

In all honesty, though, as someone has said, "Old age is not for sissies". The aging of the body often brings pain and even embarrassment. Nowhere in literature is there a more graphic picture of an aging body than in Ecclesiastes 12. The "preacher" uses figurative language to describe what it means to get old.

"The sun and the light, the moon and the stars are darkened" suggesting that impressions are less sharp than in youth. The "clouds return after the rain;" as a sickness or a pain seems to be over, only to return too soon. "The watchmen of the house (the hands) tremble." The legs grow weak and the back is bent and "mighty men stoop." When teeth are lost, "the grinding ones stand idle because they are few;" and, as the eyes fail, "those who look through windows grow dim." The doors of our homes that we exit for the day's activities, as well as the doors of opportunity that we once entered, are now "shut in the streets" and because of a loss of hearing, the "sound of the grinding mill is low."

Old age is a time when it is difficult to sleep, and "one will arise at the sound of the bird." The voice becomes weak so that "the daughters of song will sing softly;" and one is irrationally "afraid of a high place and of terrors on the road." As the hair becomes white "the almond tree blossoms;" and walking, though possible, is reminiscent of the awkward way that a "grasshopper drags himself along."

It may be that we can delay some of these handicaps for a while, but eventually the "silver cord" that binds body and soul together "is broken and the golden bowl is crushed." As the heart fails, the "wheel at the cistern is crushed" and "man goes to his eternal home while mourners go about in the street."

Other Adversities

Modern inventions have eased some of the agonies that Ecclesiastes describes. Eye glasses and surgeries may postpone blindness, and hearing aids may enable us to continue hearing with some success. New medications can lessen pain, and hair dye and wigs can conceal the blossoming of the almond tree. But there are other concerns that remain.

A group of seniors recently listed some of their vexations: being dependent on others for care and financial resources, fear of dementia, Alzheimer's, etc., death of family and friends, loneliness, the responsibility of making decisions alone, fear of irrelevance and uncertainty about ability to provide benefits to others and even to participate as a peer, concern about how their death will affect family, inability to do what we once did, and not being useful in the Lord's work. These difficulties are just as real as the failing of our physical bodies.

How we deal with the experience of aging will determine to a great degree our own personal happiness as well as the pleasure that others will have in our company.

Some Wrong Ways of Coping

Complaining is a common reaction to the burdens of age. Asking some people how they are feeling is asking for an "organ recital"—a recitation of problems with every organ of the body from the heart to the kidneys. Those who engage in such a recital then wonder why people don't want to visit them or be around them in any setting.

The use of alcohol and abuse of other drugs is too often embraced as an escape for the elderly. Research indicates that

10-15% of seniors become alcoholics who were formerly not alcoholics (Aging.com). Furthermore, 11% of elderly hospital admissions are because of drug and alcohol-related issues. The misuse of opioids is currently seen as a national crisis and seniors are especially vulnerable due to the carelessness of some doctors in prescribing and/or the failure to take the medications as prescribed.

Then there is the mistake of withdrawing from life because "I am just too old." Life expectancy has increased to the point that "old age" does not begin when it once did. We might do well to cease observing birthdays; certain milestone ages can make us feel older. After all, on any birthday, we are only one day older than we were the day before.

The Right Way to Cope

The scriptures provide us with the proper way to cope. 2 Corinthians 4:16-18 is truly a golden text for the golden aged. It is a text that should be memorized by every aging Christian, regardless of the difficulty that may be encountered in memorizing.

> Therefore, we do not lose heart. Even though our outward man is perishing, yet the inward *man* is being renewed day by day. For our light affliction, which is but for a moment, is working for us a far more exceeding *and* eternal weight of glory, while we do not look at the things which are seen, but at the things which are not seen. For the things which are seen *are* temporary, but the things which are not seen *are* eternal.

We are dual creatures having an "outward man" and an "inward man." When God created Adam, He first "formed man *of* the dust of the ground." Then He "breathed into his nostrils the breath of life; and man became a living being" (Genesis 2:7). The body and the spirit are two different entities with two different destinies. Ecclesiastes 12:7 describes what happens at death: "Then the dust will return to the earth as it was, and the spirit will return to God who gave it."

How, then can we avoid losing heart as we grow older?

First, we must learn to accept the fact that the outward man is going to perish, regardless of how hard we may try to preserve it. Understanding this, we are able to concentrate on the inward man that is eternal and can be renewed day by day.

Most of us who are Christians have convinced ourselves that we value the inward man above the outer. Perhaps we should challenge ourselves with some questions:

> 1. Which concerns me more: a physical pain or a spiritual weakness?

> 2. Which am I most concerned to protect: my body from disease or my soul from sin?

> 3. When someone asks, "How are you today?" which health do I report: the health of the outward man or the health of the inward man?

Second, we must nurture the faith that concentrates on what cannot be seen (Hebrews 11:1) rather than on what is seen. "For the things which are seen *are* temporary, but the things which are not seen *are* eternal."

Winter is Not the End

Winter may be the end of the year, but Spring will come. "While the earth remains, seedtime and harvest, cold and heat, winter and summer, and day and night shall not cease" (Genesis 8:22). And for the Christian, old age is not the end of life. A glorious and eternal springtime lies ahead.

"I consider that the sufferings of this present time are not worthy *to be compared* with the glory which shall be revealed in us" (Romans 8:18).

"And as it is appointed for men to die once, but after this the judgment, so Christ was offered once to bear the sins of many. To those who eagerly wait for Him He will appear a second time, apart from sin, for salvation" (Hebrews 9:27-28).

"When Christ *who is* our life appears, then you also will appear with Him in glory" (Colossians 3:4).

"The Lord Himself will descend from heaven with a shout, with the voice of an archangel, and with the trumpet of God. And the dead in Christ will rise first. Then we who are alive *and* remain shall be caught up together with them in the clouds to meet the Lord in the air. And thus we shall always be with the Lord" (1 Thessalonians 4:16-17).

"Beloved, now we are children of God; and it has not yet been revealed what we shall be, but we know that when He is revealed, we shall be like Him, for we shall see Him as He is" (1 John 3:2).

Examples from Scripture

God's word is peopled with examples of faith, many of them aged. These aged saints faced most of the problems that the elderly face today. "All scripture....is profitable" and what can be more profitable for aging Christians than studying the lives of those ancient examples? That is what we propose to do in the following pages. Join us for a survey of their lives in their declining years.

Wisdom is with aged men, And with length of days, understanding (Job 12:12).

Memory Work

Read over the following verses several times with a view to memorizing them. They will appear after each lesson with words missing that you should be able to fill in from memory.

"Therefore we do not lose heart. Even though our outward man is perishing, yet the inward *man* is being renewed day by day. For our light affliction, which is but for a moment, is working for us a far more exceeding *and* eternal weight of glory, while we do not look at the things which are seen, but at the things which are not seen. For the things which are seen *are* temporary, but the things which are not seen *are* eternal" (2 Corinthians 4:16-18).

Questions

1. What are some pleasant things:

About winter?

About old age?

2. Which of the marks of physical decline in Ecclesiastes 12 do you find most challenging?

Would you like to suggest a different explanation for the figures in Ecclesiastes 12 than the ones given?

3. What modern inventions help to alleviate some of the difficulties mentioned?

4. Is there any other experience not mentioned there that you find frustrating?

5. Among older people you know, what wrong way of coping do you see as the most common?

6. What are the two parts of man as described in:

Genesis 2:7

Ecclesiastes 12:7

Matthew 10:28

2 Corinthians 4:16

7. What are some exercises available to seniors that will strengthen the inner man?

8. Self-examination:

> a. On a scale of 1-10, how would you rate the health of your physical body?

> b. On a scale of 1-10, how would you rate the health of your inner man?

> c. When someone asks, "How are you?" which health do you report?

9. Do you know any older people who maintain a cheerful attitude by concentrating on the inner man?

10. Read 3rd John, verse 2. Would this be a blessing for you?

11. What fact lessens the pain of both winter and the end of life?

When peace, like a river, attendeth my way,
When sorrows like sea billows roll;
Whatever my lot, Thou hast taught me to say,
It is well, it is well with my soul.

Though Satan should buffet, though trials should come,
Let this blest assurance control,
That Christ hath regarded my helpless estate,
And hath shed His own blood for my soul.

It is well with my soul,
It is well, it is well with my soul.

Horatio G. Spafford

Chapter 2

Noah

"You have need of endurance" (Heb. 10:35).

The importance of Noah in the early history of mankind is impressive. The first eleven chapters of Genesis cover at least two thousand years of history, and Noah dominates three of those chapters. The world had become exceedingly wicked, " But Noah found grace in the eyes of the LORD" (Genesis 6:8).

Few men in all the Bible are as highly praised as Noah. "Noah was a just man, perfect (blameless, NASB) in his generations. Noah walked with God" (Genesis 6:9).

God informed Noah that the world was to be destroyed with a great flood. He was instructed to build an enormous ark for the saving of himself and his family. God gave him detailed instructions for this monumental task. And, "Thus Noah did; according to all that God commanded him, so he did" (Genesis 6:22). When the ark was completed, "the LORD said to Noah, 'Come into the ark, you and all your household, because I have seen *that* you *are* righteous before Me in this generation'" (Genesis 7:1).

It is to Noah's credit that, in what must have been the most corrupt generation in the world's history, he influenced his three sons and their wives to fear the Lord. In the New Testament, he is hailed as a hero of faith. "By faith Noah, being divinely warned of things not yet seen, moved with godly fear, prepared an ark for the saving of his household, by which he condemned the world and became heir of the righteousness which is according to faith" (Hebrews 11:7).

When the flood receded and Noah left the ark, he made a sacrifice to God. "So God blessed Noah and his sons, and said to them: 'Be fruitful and multiply, and fill the earth'" (Genesis 9:1).

What a wonderful new beginning for the world! Now, once again, all of earth's inhabitants were righteous, and the man in best position to assure its continued purity was Noah, against whom not a single word had been recorded.

Noah may have been 480 years of age when he was instructed to build the ark. But this was only middle age in his generation. His grandfather was 969 years old when he died. At 500, Noah was begetting sons (Genesis 5:32). He was 600 when the flood began, but he was still not a grandfather. He died at 950 years of age (Genesis 9:29).

But in the last third of his life, Noah tarnished his reputation with the only sin recorded in his long life.

Noah was not the only saint who damaged a good record in his later years. Of eight kings of Judah who were counted good kings, six of them in their later years sinned in a way that sullied the good record they had made in their early years. The same thing, too often, has happened to gospel preachers, diligent elders, effective teachers and other godly men and women. Let us be certain that we not allow this in our own lives.

How did Noah Sin?

"And Noah began *to be* a farmer, and he planted a vineyard. Then he drank of the wine and was drunk, and became uncovered in his tent" (Genesis 9:20-21).

It is not possible to know whether this was intentional or accidental. Was he unaware of the effect that wine would produce, or was it something he had done in the past so that it had become a habit, perhaps even an addiction? H.D.M. Spence in *Pulpit Commentary* (Genesis, p. 148) expressed his opinion that Noah was aware of the effects of wine. "Since the sin of Noah cannot be ascribed to ignorance, it is perhaps right, as well as charitable, to attribute it to age and inadvertence." Regardless, it was a sin that not only formed a blot on his record, but one that became a stumbling block to one of his sons and a curse to future generations. It is a sin to which the aged may be especially vulnerable.

Drunkenness is a Sin

"And do not be drunk with wine, in which is dissipation" (Ephesians 5:18). Galatians 5:19-21 mentions drunkenness among other sins and concludes "that those who practice such things will not inherit the kingdom of God." Jesus warned, "But take heed to yourselves, lest your hearts be weighed down with carousing, drunkenness, and cares of this life, and that Day come on you unexpectedly" (Luke 21:34).

Both in Noah's experience and in these words of Jesus, we learn the chief reason drunkenness is a sin. It is not that it makes us stagger or may result in a hangover. It is not even the effect it may have on our health. The primary reason it is a sin is that it affects our ability to think clearly. Noah did not realize he was uncovered, and, according to Jesus, those who are drunk will be taken by surprise when the Great Day comes. Absolute sobriety is needed to live the godly life and practice the watchfulness that are required of Christians.

When is one drunk? The effect on our thinking is the primary thing to be considered in answering this question. Various states have established an alcohol level at which one is too drunk to drive, but this is not the measure by which a Christian would determine drunkenness. For the Christian, it would be when one's judgment is first impaired.

The scriptures hint that older Christians are especially vulnerable to drunkenness. The "feeling of well-being" is one of the first effects of alcohol. This may offer some escape from the burdens of age, but it does not justify even a little compromise of sobriety. Titus was instructed to "speak the things which are proper for sound doctrine: that the older men be sober" (Titus 2:1-2).

William Barclay observes:

> The word is *nephalios*, and it literally means *sober* as
> opposed to given to overindulgence in wine. The point is
> that, when a man has reached years of seniority, he ought
> to have learned what are and what are not true pleasures.
> The senior men should have learned that the pleasures of
> self-indulgence cost far more than they are worth (*The
> Letters to Timothy, Titus and Philemon*, p.277).

Older women are especially urged to be "reverent in behavior,
not slanderers, not given to much wine" (Titus 2:3). Nothing
is said of wine in the instructions to be given to younger
women. This would seem to imply that age may increase the
liability to temptation.

Modern studies confirm that the elderly are especially
vulnerable to misuse of alcohol and other drugs which
produce the same effects.

> Drug and alcohol abuse among the elderly is a rapidly
> growing health problem in the United States. There are
> several things that could contribute to someone turning to
> substance abuse later in life. These could be health-related
> issues or life-changing events that take an emotional toll.
> These events may provoke drug-abusing behavior that can
> result in a full-scale addiction. Potential triggers for drug or
> alcohol addiction in the elderly are:
>
> • Retirement

- Death of a family member, spouse, pet, or close friend

- Loss of income or financial strain

- Relocation or placement in a nursing home

- Trouble sleeping

- Family conflict

- Mental or physical health decline (depression, memory loss, major surgeries, etc.)

  https://www.addictioncenter.com/addiction   Jan. 26.2019

Medicinal Use

A common argument to justify the use of alcohol for medicinal purpose is Paul's advice to Timothy, "No longer drink only water, but use a little wine for your stomach's sake and your frequent infirmities" (1 Timothy 5:23).

Paul's instruction was to use "a little" for his "stomach's sake," not for dulling the mental awareness of his problem. Today, we have much more effective stomach remedies as well as remedies for other disorders for which wine is sometimes used.

Rather often we see claims that a moderate use of wine is healthy. A recent study in England, reported by Ryan W.

Miller in USA Today (April 5, 2019), states otherwise. "Just one to two drinks a day can increase risk of high blood pressure and stroke, a new study found, debunking the myth that moderate alcohol consumption could protect against those risks."

One thing clearly implied in the text cited is that Timothy was not using any wine at all, even if it might have been useful. We should be advised by Timothy's good example to avoid the use of alcohol completely in view of the dangers involved.

If one should avoid alcohol because of its effect on our ability to think clearly, then all mind-altering drugs become suspect. In addition, one cannot afford the risk of addiction that accompanies the use of many drugs.

What about mind-altering prescription drugs? Paul's advice to Timothy would seem to justify the use of those that are prescribed for specific disorders if nothing better is available. But even these are dangerous. They need to be used for correction of some specific condition or to aid in healing, not just for the good feeling they produce.

Some doctors are careless about prescribing drugs simply because patients request them, and the requests all too often are generated by an addiction rather than genuine need. Even the prescriptions of careful physicians can be misused. The misuse may be unintentional, but the results can be the same. Those who become addicted often take more than is prescribed and seek the same prescription from different doctors.

Christian patients should inform doctors of their strong desire to avoid addiction. "All things are lawful for me, but all things are not helpful. All things are lawful for me, **but I will not be brought under the power of any**"(1 Corinthians 6:12).

According to a 2009 SAMHSA National Survey on Drug use and Health, there are significant increases in illicit drug use in the aging population. This includes nonmedical use of prescription drugs among those over age 60. Alchohol was the most frequently reported with opiates as the second (https://www.addictionhope.com/blog/connections-drug-abuse-aging).

An internet article states:

> As a whole, more older men have substance abuse problems than do older women, but women are more likely than men to start drinking heavily later in life. Substance abuse is more prevalent among persons who suffer a number of losses, including death of loved ones, retirement, and loss of health. The fact that women are more likely to be widowed or divorced, to have experienced depression, and to have been prescribed psychoactive medications that increase the negative effects of alcohol help explain these gender differences.
>
> https://www.hazeldenberryfood.org/articles/substance-abuse (Jan. 26, 2019)

A Christian who becomes aware of an increasing dependence on a particular mind-altering drug should seek the help of a physician to withdraw. A Christian woman of our acquaintance suffered a serious psychosis following a botched surgery. She was totally out of her mind and obviously needed something to calm her. A psychiatrist placed her on a powerful tranquilizer, intending to decrease it as the crisis passed, but before he could begin the reduction he died. Other physicians were reluctant to undertake to help with withdrawal and the patient continued for years almost a zombie. One doctor who undertook to help was incompetent and she almost died in his office. Finally, a skilled physician was asked to help. He agreed to do so but, knowing how difficult it would be, he expressed his doubts that she would tolerate the withdrawal symptoms. He underestimated the determination of his Christian patient. She did endure the withdrawal for the required time, and she returned to the vivacious personality she had been in the past. It can be done.

The Influence on Others

The curse of Noah's drunkenness on his family has been duplicated in families throughout the centuries. As Bill and Judy Norris observe in their book, *What the Bible Says About Growing Old,* "Reverence and respect are fragile commodities. Noah had spent a lifetime building a reputation for wisdom and morality. He blew it with one of his sons in one unguarded moment" (page 23).

Our descendants may not do what Ham did, but sadness has invaded many a home because of the misuse of alcohol by a father or mother. And the practice of alcohol and drug abuse tends to recur from generation to generation. It is difficult for a child to see the dangers of actions that they have seen practiced by respected parents and grandparents. Surely this is reason enough to avoid any practice that could become a stumbling block to our children and grandchildren.

> Do not look on the wine when it is red,
> When it sparkles in the cup,
> When it swirls around smoothly;
> At the last it bites like a serpent,
> And stings like a viper (Proverbs 23:31-32).

Memory Work

Read over the following verses several time with a view to memorizing them. They will appear after each lesson with words missing which you should be able to fill in from memory.

"Therefore we do not lose heart. Even though our _____ _____ man is perishing, yet the inward *man* is being renewed day by day. For our light affliction, which is but for a moment, is working for us a far more exceeding *and* eternal weight of glory, while we do not look at the things which are seen, but at the things which are not seen. For the things which are seen *are* temporary, but the things which are not seen *are* eternal (2 Corinthians 4:16-18).

Questions

1. What makes the character of Noah so remarkable in his early years?

a. What is meant by "Perfect (blameless) in his generations?"

b. Does this suggest that God may judge us in the context of our generation?

2. How old was Noah when he died? How did he tarnish his image in the last third of his life?

3. What advantages do we have in our generation that Noah did not have?

4. Has God asked us to do anything as challenging as building the ark as He designed it?

5. What did Noah accomplish with his family?

What does this teach us about the possibility of rearing faithful children, even in our evil generation?

6. What effect did his sin have on his family?

7. What habits of ours can affect our families

a. For their harm?

b. For their good?

8. Why do you think God has designated drunkenness as a sin?

At what point would drinking become a sin?

9. What are some things that tempt aging Christians to turn to alcohol and other drugs?

10. What are the alternatives available to Christians for dealing with these?

11. What word in Titus 2:2 would require older men to abstain from anything that would affect their judgment?

12. How does Titus 2:3-5 imply that older women may be more tempted to alcohol than younger women?

13. What precautions should all Christians take, even with prescription drugs?

Chapter 3

Jacob

"So his sons did for him just as he had commanded them" (Genesis 50:12).

When a president meets with the leader of another country, it is a major news event. Such a meeting is reported in Genesis, chapter 47, but the news media of that day took no notice. True, the most powerful king on earth was involved. But who could have dreamed that the old shepherd who was introduced to the king was a patriarch whose God-given name, Israel, would identify a race of people who would continue for thousands of years.

"Then Joseph brought in his father Jacob and set him before Pharaoh; and Jacob blessed Pharaoh" (verse 7).

"Jacob blessed Pharaoh." The Hebrew writer observes: "Now beyond all contradiction the lesser is blessed by the better" (Hebrews 7:7). Whether Pharaoh realized the significance of this event or not, it is certainly true that this saint of God was superior to him who was merely king of Egypt. Rulers even today are blessed when unknown saints, young or old, offer "supplications, prayers, intercessions, *and* giving of thanks…for all who are in authority" (1 Tim. 2:1-2).

One translation (ESV) says "They stood him before Pharaoh." If this translation is correct, one might wonder why he stood instead of bowing as would have been expected. Was it the respect Pharaoh had for Joseph that did not demand a bow from his father? Or was it, perhaps, that if he bowed at his age, he might not be able to get up? Those of us who are older realize the danger of bowing too low. An aged preacher, when commended for his erect posture replied, "Sister, if I bent over even slightly, I'd fall flat on my face."

Be that as it may, it is apparent that Pharaoh was impressed with Jacob's age. "Pharaoh said to Jacob, "How old *are* you?" (verse 8). It is understandable that Pharaoh was impressed. There is evidence that in Egypt, 110 was considered the maximum age that anyone might hope to attain. No wonder, then, Pharaoh asked old Jacob, "How old are you?"

How old are you? Different people answer in different ways. Children love to tell you how old they'll be their next birthday. Becoming a teenager is a milestone of which young people boast. Then come the years when most people would rather not talk about it; some even lie about it. Finally, the time comes again when we tell how old we'll be "if I reach my next birthday." Maybe that's the reason some call it "second childhood."

Jacob's answer was unique. "And Jacob said to Pharaoh, 'The days of the years of my pilgrimage *are* one hundred and thirty years; few and evil have been the days of the years of my life, and they have not attained to the days of the years of the life of my fathers in the days of their pilgrimage'" (verse 9).

If Pharaoh was impressed with Jacob's great age, Jacob was not. "Few and evil have been the days of the years of my life," was his response. He considered his years few because he was comparing their number with that of his ancestors. His grandfather had lived to be 175 and his father 180. Measured by their ages, Jacob was comparatively young. In our generation life expectancy has increased. The World Health Organization has done new research recently based on health quality and life expectancy and defined a new criterion that divides human age as follows: 0-17 years old: underage; 18-65 years old: youth or young people; 66 to 79 years old: middle aged; 80-99 years old: elderly or senior; 100+ years old: long-lived elderly. Perhaps we should forget the old standards and realize that we are not as old as we think we are. Or, perhaps, that we are *only* as old as we think we are.

Jacob also observed that the "years of his pilgrimage" had been "evil." We might say today that he had a lot of hard mileage on him. Perhaps Jacob was referring to the suffering he had endured, much of it brought on by his own deceitful dealings. In addition, however, he had also been the object of deception again and again. The deception that brought him most grief was the deception that led him to believe for 22 years that his favorite son had been killed by a wild beast. Then, too, there had been the famine in Canaan and the anxiety he had suffered as he struggled with the decision to allow his youngest son to be taken to Egypt. Suffering does indeed age us and make life seem longer. Perhaps we should consider "the mileage" when judging the appearance of a friend whose body seems prematurely aged.

But suffering, even into old age, does not necessarily have to continue, especially if the "inward man is being renewed day by day." Jacob's inner man had been renewed. This saintly Jacob at 130 years, who "worshiped, leaning on his staff" (Hebrews 11:21), was a different Jacob from the deceiver of earlier years. His encounter with God, as he prepared to meet his brother Esau, was a turning point in his life. Now the tide had turned. He was not only a better man, but he had seen Joseph for whom he had grieved so long, and Joseph was now his caregiver. His sons were changed. Judah, the very one who had proposed that Joseph be sold, had offered himself as a slave in order to assure the return of Benjamin. And Jacob was now being provided with the best Egypt had to offer. Indeed, the last 17 years of his life were not "evil".

Concerning those 17 years, "Israel said to Joseph, 'I had not thought to see your face; but in fact, God has also shown me your offspring'" (Genesis 48:11). "Children's children *are* the crown of old men, and the glory of children *is* their father" (Proverbs 17:6).

The unpleasant experiences of our past life do not necessarily continue into our later years. Like Jacob, we may be able to turn over a new leaf and live out the remainder of our lives more pleasantly. Let us not dwell on the past to the point that we fail to see the good things life is offering us now.

Jacob's Preparations for Death

As we grow older our relationship with our adult children changes. After spending years caring and providing for them, we become increasingly dependent on them. We can make that care more difficult or easier. Jacob did at least three things that were helpful to his children in his later years

First, he moved to be near his primary caregiver (Genesis 45:9-13). Joseph, due to his access to the abundant food supply in Egypt, was in better position to take care of his aged father than any of his brothers in Canaan where the famine was to last another 5 years. When Joseph sent for Jacob to come to Egypt Jacob could have said, "I am too old to make such a long journey. Let Joseph come and take care of me or arrange for servants to come and bring supplies as they are needed." It was, indeed, a long journey, especially for a 130 year old man, but Jacob did not hesitate. He inconvenienced himself to make it more convenient for his caregiver.

Second, Jacob informed his children of his burial preferences. He called for Joseph and said, "Please do not bury me in Egypt, but let me lie with my fathers; you shall carry me out of Egypt and bury me in their burial place" (Genesis 47:29-30). Later, when all of his sons were gathered, "he charged them and said to them: 'I am to be gathered to my people; bury me with my fathers in the cave that *is* in the field of Ephron the Hittite, in the cave that *is* in the field of Machpelah, which *is* before Mamre in the land of Canaan, which Abraham bought with the field of Ephron the Hittite as a possession for a burial place'" (Genesis 49:29-30).

Third, he did everything possible to prevent strife among his children after he was gone. He made clear which of his children should have the birthright, a double portion of the inheritance. Normally, it would have gone to the oldest, but the birthright was taken from Reuben and given to Joseph. By choosing to give each of Joseph's two sons an equal inheritance with his own sons, he was giving Joseph twice the inheritance of the others, the right of primogeniture (Genesis 48:22). Then, to make sure that Reuben knew why he was not given that right, Jacob stated the reason in the presence of all the sons (Genesis 49:3-4). This was tantamount to making a will.

Furthermore, if the brothers are to be believed, Jacob did what he could to prevent the opening of old wounds related to their mistreatment of Joseph. "They sent *messengers* to Joseph, saying, 'Before your father died he commanded, saying, "Thus you shall say to Joseph: 'I beg you, please forgive the trespass of your brothers and their sin; for they did evil to you.' Now, please, forgive the trespass of the servants of the God of your father" (Genesis 50:16-17).

Practical Lessons for Us

Regardless of how much we desire to complete our lives caring for ourselves, it usually is not possible. Sooner or later, we must depend on others. Our children have the first responsibility (1 Timothy 5:4, 8, 16) and godly children are eager to fulfill that duty. But whose convenience should come first—ours or theirs? If children live at some distance from us, our insistence on remaining in our home may place an unreasonable burden on them. They must either interrupt their lives again and again in order to travel to our side, or allow non-family members to do what godly children feel that they should be doing. The logical solution is for us to move to be as close as possible to our caregivers.

An older couple of our acquaintance lived more than 275 miles from their nearest daughter. She was having to disrupt her life constantly to make the long trip to help with some crisis in their lives. They decided to uproot from their native area and move to be near their daughter. Not only did they enable her to give them better care and to do it more easily, but they became virtual grandparents to the many younger couples in the church where she worshiped.

Yes, the older we are the more difficult such a move will be, but it will be no more difficult than the move that Jacob made in a wagon from Canaan to Egypt, and few of us are 130 years old.

All too often, the death of a parent, especially the last one surviving, creates tensions among the children. Sometimes, selfish children want everything done according to their wishes and expect more than their share of what is left. Even unselfish children whose desire is to carry out the wishes of their deceased parents may disagree about what the parents' preferences would have been. Some foresight on the part of the parents can do much to prevent such tensions.

Parents should give their children some direction as to how their decease should be handled. We may selfishly say, "It makes no difference to me; I won't be aware." That's true, but a failure to offer some direction creates the possibility for serious disagreement among the most loving children at a time when emotion makes them more vulnerable to disagreements and hurt feelings. A living will is appropriate, so that children will know what heroic efforts we desire to keep us alive even after nature decrees our death. Then, do we desire to be buried or cremated? If buried, where? What kind of funeral do we desire? No matter how detailed our instructions are, our children will still have many decisions to make. It is our duty to make it as easy for them as possible.

A will is the least we can do to help our children navigate the complexity of distributing what we leave. Without a will, in most states the courts will determine how our assets are distributed and it may not be where we would desire. Underage children may even be placed in undesirable homes. When our estate is relatively simple, a will can be made on the internet with a minimum of time and expense.

Finally, letters to each of our children expressing our love for them and urging their love for one another will have special weight with them after we are gone. After all, is that not the message that Jesus left with His disciples as He was preparing to leave them? "This is My commandment, that you love one another as I have loved you" (John 15:12).

Whatever we intend to do along these lines should not be delayed but considered urgent. A local commercial for a security system ends, "It's better to be a month too early than one day too late." And so it is with these preparations for the end.

> You do not know what will happen tomorrow.
> For what is your life? It is even a vapor that appears for a little time and then vanishes away (James 4:14).

Memory Work

Fill in the blanks from memory:

> Therefore we do not lose heart. Even though our _____ ___ man is perishing, yet the _____ *man* is being renewed day by day. For our light affliction, which is but for a moment, is working for us a far more exceeding *and* eternal weight of glory, while we do not look at the things which are seen, but at the things which are not seen. For the things which are seen *are* temporary, but the things which are not seen *are* eternal.

Questions

1. Jacob blessed Pharaoh. What are some ways that we can bless rulers (See Romans 13:7; 1 Timothy 2:1-4; 1 Peter 2:17)?

2. Pharaoh and Jacob apparently felt differently about Jacob's age. What are some things that determine how old we consider ourselves?

3. Jacob considered his days "evil."

    a. Why were his earlier days evil?

    b. Were his later years "evil"?

    c. What made the difference?

    d. What are some things we can do to change the quality of our lives even in old age? (Remember our memory verses.)

4. What did Jacob do to make it easier for the caregiver who was in best position to help him? Whose convenience should have priority—ours or our caregiver's?

5. What can we do to assure that someone is responsible for attending to our business if we become incapable of doing so?

6.. Why is it important to let our children know our preferences for our death arrangements?

What arrangements can we make in advance for ourselves? *Note: It is often unwise to prepay funerals or to buy cemetery lots too far in advance.*

If children are uncomfortable discussing it, we can at least leave written instructions.

7.What are some things we can do to discourage strife among our children involving the material things we leave behind?

8.What did Joshua do as death approached (Joshua 23-24)?

9. "In those days Hezekiah was sick and near death. And Isaiah the prophet, the son of Amoz, went to him and said to him, "Thus says the LORD: 'Set your house in order, for you shall die and not live.' " (Isaiah 38:1). List some things that you might need to do to set your house in order.

    a.

    b.

    c.

    d.

10. What did Jesus do when he knew death was near (John 13-17)?

Chapter 4

Moses

"By faith, Moses—" (Hebrews 11:23).

Other than Jesus, Moses is the most universally honored character found in the pages of the Bible. He wrote more of the Bible than any other author. His name appears in the New Testament more often than that of any other Old Testament character. Even in the Koran, his name appears more often than any other. There is a large statue of him in the Library of Congress and there are carvings representing him in the Supreme Court building. He has a statue in the House of Representatives which is in the center of twenty-three with all the others looking toward him.

And it all began at the age of eighty!

It also began in an extraordinary way. An eighty-year old shepherd was with his sheep in the wilderness when he saw a remarkable sight. A bush was burning, but it was not consumed. God spoke to him out of that bush and commissioned him to go to Egypt and deliver His people from their slavery. Understandably, Moses was taken back by the challenge of such a task. He began immediately making excuses: "Who am I? Who shall I say sent me? They won't believe me. I am not a good speaker."

The one excuse he did not make is the one most of us would have expected: "I'm too old."

He was not too old. In fact, he was persuaded to do what God sent him to do. He served as God's agent to liberate Israel from slavery and bring them out of Egypt. Then, for the next forty years, he led approximately two million people through that very wilderness where he had met God, all the way to the border of the land God had promised to their ancestors.

But really, did it all begin at eighty? He could not have done what he did at eighty had it not been for the events of the preceding years.

The Value of Previous Experiences

The story of his rescue by Pharaoh's daughter when he was an infant, and his adoption as her son is well known. Providentially, his own mother was employed to be his nurse for the first few years of his life and, by the time he left her care, he was aware of his identity as an Israelite and knew of Israel's God. In Pharaoh's palace, "Moses was learned in all the wisdom of the Egyptians, and was mighty in words and deeds" (Acts 7:22). But after using his own devices in an aborted effort to lead his people from their slavery, he had to flee the country to escape Pharaoh's wrath; and he spent the next forty years following the lowly occupation of a shepherd.

But think how those first eighty years were necessary in order to do what God sent him to do. Had he not had the training of his mother, he would not have known of Israel's God. Had he not spent those forty years in Pharaoh's court, he would have been totally intimidated when he returned to that very court to demand release of his people. And had he not spent those forty years in "that great and terrible wilderness, in which were fiery serpents and scorpions" (Deuteronomy 8:15), he could not have endured its hardships to lead God's people through it to the promised land.

Bill and Judy Norris express it this way.

> The forty years of early education had fortified Moses with deep faith plus a knowledge and refinement guaranteed to produce respect from his hearers whether they were the elders of Israel or the courtiers of the king. His forty years of solitude and meditation had calmed his tempestuous spirit, enabling him to bear up under the stresses of leadership with a slave mentality people. Those wilderness years had also equipped him with the ability to live under nomadic deprivations (*"What the Bible Says about Growing Old"* p.50).

In our own life, the experiences we have had and the skills we have learned in our earlier years can be used for the Lord at the time of retirement. What a pity that some consider

retirement from secular duties the time to retire from the
Lord's service.

When C. T. Jones had an opportunity to transfer to London,
near the end of his career with Exxon, he accepted the offer
in view of opportunities it offered to serve the Lord. During
most of the time he was in England, he very effectively taught
the Sunday morning Bible class at the Kentish Town church
and served also to assist American preachers who came to
work in England. He retired in England and when he returned
to the United States he had to decide where he would live
and what he would do. He could have purchased an RV and
traveled, or he could have moved to a retirement community
and spent his time in recreation. Rather, he decided to move
back to his own home town of Lawrenceburg, Tennessee,
where his aged father needed care and where the church
desperately needed leadership. Since he was already well-known
in Lawrenceburg, he was very soon appointed an elder and
he began immediately to use for the Lord the expertise he
had gained at Exxon. In London, he had been responsible for
predicting the oil requirements of various European countries
into the next century. Johnny Felker, who was preaching in
Lawrenceburg at the time, reported, "Using those skills, he
has shown a remarkable ability to analyze a situation and
then implement workable solutions to those problems. By
delegating responsibility to faithful men in many areas, the
elders have been able to focus more on the spiritual needs of
the congregation." In reality, the church had another full-time,
though unpaid, worker.

The Value of Succession Training

Some time ago, a friend told me of a program his company had implemented called Succession Planning. Supervisors and managers were required to identify younger employees who showed qualities of leadership. These were to be given special assignments and trained in various ways so that they would be ready when their superiors retired.

Whether Moses was that far ahead of his time or if God simply led him to do it, his was a good example of succession training. According to the NASB translation of Numbers 11:28, Joshua the son of Nun was *"the attendant of Moses from his youth."*

Soon after Israel left Egypt, "Amalek came and fought with Israel in Rephidim. And Moses said to Joshua, "Choose us some men and go out, fight with Amalek." Moses gave support by standing on the top of the hill with the upraised rod of God in his hand. This was essential to the victory that was gained, but Moses showed no resentment when it was recorded that "Joshua defeated Amalek and his people with the edge of the sword." It was Moses, in fact, who wrote that report (Exodus 17:8-13). How different this was from the reaction of Saul when David was credited with victory over the Philistines.

When Moses ascended Mt. Sinai to receive the law, Joshua went up partway with him and apparently waited the 40 days until Moses returned (Exodus 24:13-18, 32:17).

When Moses was not allowed to enter the promised land, Joshua was well prepared to assume the leadership of God's people. And when God informed Moses that Joshua was to be his successor, "Moses called Joshua and said to him in the sight of all Israel, 'Be strong and of good courage, for you must go with this people to the land which the Lord has sworn to their fathers to give them, and you shall cause them to inherit it. And the Lord, He is the One who goes before you. He will be with you, He will not leave you nor forsake you; do not fear nor be dismayed'" (Deuteronomy 31:7-8). Again, how different this reaction from that of Saul when he realized that David was to be his successor.

The example of Moses should be a strong incentive to Christians who fill various roles in the church to plan for the future by training successors. For example, we knew a church where one good man led all the singing for many years. When he moved away, no one else had been prepared to lead singing and the church suffered from it. We are foolish to think that we will be here forever; who will carry on when we are gone? We must prepare ourselves for the immediate coming of the Lord, but we must prepare others for the possibility that He will delay.

The Value of Knowing When to Retire

Although Moses graciously accepted God's choice of a successor, he was very reluctant to retire. The conversation between God and Moses recorded in Deuteronomy 3:23-26 still tugs at our heart strings. This old soldier, now 120 years

of age, is almost to the destination of which he has dream
He reports,

> Then I pleaded with the Lord at that time, saying: "O
> Lord God, You have begun to show Your servant Your
> greatness and Your mighty hand, for what god is there
> in heaven or on earth who can do anything like Your
> works and Your mighty deeds? I pray, let me cross over
> and see the good land beyond the Jordan, those pleasant
> mountains, and Lebanon." But the Lord was angry with
> me on your account, and would not listen to me. So the
> Lord said to me: "Enough of that! Speak no more to Me
> of this matter."

It is never easy to give up a work that one loves, especially
when there are goals that have not yet been achieved. But that
time comes for all of us. Better to give brethren an example of
graceful retirement than to insist on continuing in whatever role
we may have served until we become more of a hindrance than
an asset to the cause of the Lord. It is a good practice to request
family members or a trusted friend to advise us when it is time
to begin our journey up Mount Nebo and turn over our rod of
leadership to some waiting Joshua.

The Value of Grace

It seems almost cruel that Moses was not allowed to enter
the land of which he had dreamed for so long. However, it
was because of unbelief that the majority of Israelites were
not allowed to enter (Hebrews 3:19); and Moses himself was

guilty of unbelief when he failed to give God glory for the water that flowed from the rock in Kadesh (Numbers 20:12). He had surely been forgiven, but this was the temporal consequence of his sin.

How do we know he was forgiven? He appeared with Elijah and Jesus in the most illustrious summit conference in the world's history (Matthew 17:1-8). And the saints in heaven sing the song of Moses and the Lamb (Revelation 15:3-4). One moment after entering the heavenly Canaan, his disappointment at not entering the earthly one must have been instantly forgotten.

The sins we commit in our lifetime can be forgiven. They are forgiven when, as penitent sinners, we are baptized and our sins are washed away (Acts 22:16). This baptism puts us into Christ (Galatians 3:27). "In Him we have redemption through His blood, the forgiveness of sins, according to the riches of His grace" (Ephesians 1:7). Physical, social, and mental consequences may remain as result of our sins, but once they are forgiven, as was the sin of Moses, there are no eternal consequences to follow. This is the penalty that Christ removed for Moses and for all true believers.

The steps of a good man are ordered by the Lord,
And He delights in his way.
Though he fall, he shall not be utterly cast down;
For the Lord upholds him with His hand (Psalm 37:23-24).

Memory Work

Fill in the blanks from memory:

Therefore we do not lose heart. Even though our _____man is
_____, yet the _____ man is being _____day by day.
For our light affliction, which is but for a moment, is working
for us a far more exceeding and eternal weight of glory, while we
do not look at the things which are seen, but at the things which
are not seen. For the things which are seen are temporary, but the
things which are not seen are eternal (2 Corinthians 4:16-18).

Questions

1. What would have been lost if Moses had insisted on
retiring at age 65?

2. What excuses did Moses give when God called him to
deliver Israel?

    a.

    b.

    c.

    d.

Are you ever tempted to offer these or similar excuses for
not doing some good work?

3. How did the following experiences in early life prepare him for his life's work for the Lord?

    a. His life in Pharaoh's court?

    b. His life as a shepherd?

4. What experiences in your early life can be useful to you in serving the Lord as you age?

5. What advice did Moses' father-in-law give him in Exodus 18:13-27?

    a. Did Moses follow his advice?   What quality did this require in Moses?

    b. What are some circumstances in which we might need this lesson?

6. What can the following persons do to prepare younger people for service in the future?

    a. Parents?

    b. Evangelists?

    c. Elders?

    d. Song Leaders?

e. Older women (Titus 2:4-5)?

7. How can aging Christians determine when it is time to turn over their duties to others?

8. Why was Moses not permitted to enter the promised land?

9. How can the example of Moses comfort us when we suffer consequences of past sins?

10. What thought can console us when we face the fact that we are too old for some experience we long to enjoy?

Chapter 5

Caleb

"Give me this mountain" (Joshua 14:12) .

S peaking of his advanced age, an old farmer once said to me, "I don't make any plans for the future." I thought to myself, "Now that's old." Later, when a friend reported, "I don't buy any green bananas," I thought to myself, "He may be joking, but that's **really** old."

Age is best judged, not by years or even by physical strength, but by attitude. Judged by attitude, Caleb remained young until he died, probably about the same age as the old farmer.

A Man of a Different Spirit

The first mention of Caleb was when the Israelites had reached the border of Canaan. They had spent one year at Mt. Sinai and now they were just two years out of Egypt. Twelve spies were sent to view the land promised to their forefathers. Caleb, at the age of forty, was chosen to represent the tribe of Judah. On their return, the spies were enthusiastic in praise of the land. Indeed, it was "a land flowing with milk and honey" as it had been described. But ten of the spies were alarmed by the fortifications of the cities and the size of the people. They noted particularly the inhabitants of the mountains around Hebron: "There we saw the giants (the descendants of Anak came from the giants); and we were like grasshoppers in our own sight, and so we were in their sight" (Numbers 13:33). Two spies, Joshua and Caleb, insisted that they could conquer the land. However, the ten fearful spies so terrified the rest of the people that they despaired of going farther and even talked of returning to Egypt.

God was so highly displeased with His people that He decreed that, except for Joshua and Caleb, none of those who were numbered who were over twenty years of age when they left Egypt would enter Canaan; all would die in the wilderness. However, God made a significant statement about Caleb: "But My servant Caleb, because he has a different spirit in him and has followed Me fully, I will bring into the land where he went, and his descendants shall inherit it" (Numbers 14:24).

That "different spirit" was evident throughout Caleb's life. Evidently, by nature, he was positive, optimistic, enthusiastic and courageous. But it was not for this reason that he encouraged his fellows to enter the land; it was his faith in God. He said,

> If the Lord delights in us, then He will bring us into this land and give it to us, 'a land which flows with milk and honey.' Only do not rebel against the Lord, nor fear the

people of the land, for they are our bread; their protection has departed from them, and the Lord is with us. Do not fear them" (Numbers 14:8-9).

Thirty-eight Years in the Wilderness

For thirty-eight more years, Caleb wandered with Moses in the wilderness. He marked his fiftieth birthday; then his sixtieth, and seventieth and probably his seventy-eighth. All of this time, those his age were dying: some in plagues, some in war, some by stoning, some by fire from heaven, and some perhaps from natural causes. By the time he was eighty, he and Joshua were twenty years older than most of their peers. They must have seemed aged indeed.

Being older than anyone around you is enough to make you feel aged. There a sense of isolation as you realize that there is no one around you who has shared the experiences of your earlier life.

Imagine the amazement of those younger people when Moses, just before he died, repeated the promise that old Caleb and his children would receive "the land on which he walked, because he wholly followed the Lord." (Deuteronomy 1:36).

The Conquest of Canaan

Caleb's confidence that God could give Israel the land was fully justified. Under the leadership of Joshua, they swept through the land with the irresistible power of a hurricane. God made city walls to crumble, hailstones to fall and even the sun and the moon to stand still. Summarizing their conquest: "So Joshua took the whole land, according to all that the Lord had said to Moses; and Joshua gave it as an inheritance to Israel according to their divisions by their tribes" (Joshua 11:23).

The exact order of the conquest is not entirely clear. Furthermore, since Israel was not able to populate all the conquered land immediately, some of the conquered people apparently returned to their former homes. Regardless of the reason, seven years after the entry to Canaan, the giants, known as the Anakim, that the spies had so much dreaded, were still (or again) in the region around Hebron. This was the very portion of land that God had promised Caleb.

"Give Me this Mountain"

Joshua 14 records Caleb's approach to Joshua to claim his inheritance. "Now therefore, give me this mountain of which the Lord spoke in that day" (vs. 12).

Very likely the younger people around Caleb were startled at this request. There were so many reasons he should not undertake it. For one thing, he was eighty-five years old (vs. 10). There were those giants and fortified cities (vs. 12). If the spies had felt that the armies of Israel could not conquer them, how could old Caleb propose to do so.

But Caleb had "a different spirit in him." He offered at least three reasons for undertaking the conquest.

First, he was still physically strong. "As yet I am as strong this day as on the day that Moses sent me; just as my strength was then, so now is my strength for war, both for going out and for coming in" (vs. 11).

Second, "Moses swore on that day, saying, 'Surely the land where your foot has trodden shall be your inheritance and your children's forever, because you have wholly followed the Lord my God.'" (vs. 9). He did not expect it "on a silver platter" but if God promised it, it was obtainable.

Third, he was not depending on human strength, but on God. This was the plea he had made to the rebellious Israelites at Kadesh, "the Lord is with us. Do not fear them" (Numbers 14:8-9). Now, he gives God the glory for preserving him to his advanced age: "Behold, the Lord has kept me alive, as He said, these forty-five years, ever since the Lord spoke this word to Moses while Israel wandered in the wilderness; and now, here I am this day, eighty-five years old" (vs. 10). And it was the basis of his confidence that he could take "this mountain." "It may be that the Lord will be with me, and I shall be able to drive them out as the Lord said" (vs. 12).

Caleb Needed Help

"This mountain" was more than one mere peak; it was a mountain range that reached ten to twelve miles to the South and included the city of Debir.

"Caleb drove out the three sons of Anak from there [Hebron]: Sheshai, Ahiman, and Talmai, the children of Anak. Then he went up from there to the inhabitants of Debir." (Joshua 15:14-15).

When Caleb contemplated taking Debir (Kirjath Sepher), he apparently felt the need of help. "And Caleb said, 'He who attacks Kirjath Sepher and takes it, to him I will give Achsah my daughter as wife'" (Joshua 15:16). A man by the name of Othniel volunteered and became Caleb's son-in-law.

This seems to add a dimension to Caleb's character: he was humble. It takes a certain amount of humility to admit that we need help. But there comes a time when anyone, especially one who is even approaching the age of eighty-five, needs help. It is pride that keeps us from asking for help when we should, and often our delay only increases the load for those who must come eventually to our aid.

It is interesting to note that Othniel, who assisted Caleb, eventually became the first judge of Israel in that long line of judges that ended with Samuel. Doubtless, the experience gained under the direction of Caleb and the influence of that good father-in-law helped to prepare him for that more important task of judging Israel.

Some Practical Questions

Is it right to undertake a task that one may not be able to see through to the end? Before answering that question, perhaps we should remember that no one, young or old, can be sure of finishing any task that is begun.

> Come now, you who say, "Today or tomorrow we will go to such and such a city, spend a year there, buy and sell, and make a profit"; whereas you do not know what will happen tomorrow. For what is your life? It is even a vapor that appears for a little time and then vanishes away. Instead you ought to say, "If the Lord wills, we shall live and do this or that." But now you boast in your arrogance. All such boasting is evil (James 4:13-16).

Is it wrong to undertake a task for which we may not be adequate? The answer to this one may not be quite so clear. Humility should remind us that any task could prove impossible due to unforeseen complications. If something needs to be done and there are others better qualified to do it, we should be happy to have them do it. But if no one is available or willing to do it, we should not let it go undone because of our feelings of inadequacy. Faith should give us the courage to proceed. "I can do all things through Christ who strengthens me" (Philippians 4:13).

Is it a sign of weakness to ask for help? Laziness maybe, but not necessarily weakness. Like Caleb, we should be humble enough to acknowledge that a project has become too big for us. Like Caleb, we should then ask for help. And, like Caleb, we should offer some reward for those to whom we make our appeal. We may not offer a daughter, but maybe a prayer, a word of encouragement, or anything that will show our gratitude. And, like Othniel, those we recruit may actually benefit from the opportunity to help. "Remember the words of the Lord Jesus, that He said, 'It is more blessed to give than to receive'" (Acts 20:35).

> "I will lift up my eyes to the hills—
> From whence comes my help?
> My help comes from the Lord,
> Who made heaven and earth (Psalm 121:1-2).

A Modern Caleb

A widow of our acquaintance, in her late sixties, had a great grandson who needed care. No one else was available to do what was needed. She began almost from his infancy to care for him and, as time passed, she became his constant caregiver. When her right to have him was contested, she went to court to obtain guardianship, concerned not for herself but for the well-being of the child.

Many felt she was undertaking too much, and some were even critical. "She's too old to take on a little one. It will be too much of a responsibility. Her final years will be dominated by the burden of rearing a child. Suppose she dies before he's mature? Who will provide the male influence he will need in his life?" Others were concerned for her; she was concerned for the boy. She was not unaware of these complications and she struggled with some of them too, but the child needed care that only she was in position to give him. It was something that had to be done.

Compelled by love for the child and reassured by her faith in God's help, she undertook a mountain of responsibility. It was a confining undertaking, but she never complained. And, in remarkable ways God did provide help as she needed it. Christian friends stood by her as she reared him "in the nurture and admonition of the Lord". One of her grandsons, an uncle of the child, gradually entered the child's life and provided the male influence that was needed. As the boy reached his teens he moved into the home of the uncle with grandmother in an adjoining apartment.

She died suddenly at the age of eighty-five. Just a year later, her great-grandson graduated from high school with the highest honors possible, both for academic achievement and for moral character. Even after "retirement age," she had conquered her mountain, and "her works do follow her."

Memory Work

Fill in the blanks from memory:

> Therefore we do not lose heart. Even though our _____
> _ man is _____, yet the _____ man is being
> _____ day by day. For our light affliction, which is
> but for a moment, is working for us a far more exceeding
> and eternal weight of glory, while we do not look at the
> things which are seen, but at the things which are not
> seen. For the things which are seen are _____,
> but the things which are not seen are _____ (2
> Corinthians 4:16-18).

Questions

1. When Moses sent out spies as Israel approached Canaan, what discouraging fact did they report on their return?

2. What did they identify as the most unconquerable part of the land?

3. On what basis did Caleb insist that the Israelites could conquer the land?

4. What did God state as the consequences of Israel's lack of faith?

5. Who were the exceptions?

6. What was Caleb promised?

7. How old was Caleb when he requested his mountain?

8. What three reasons did he give for believing he could take that portion of land?

    a.

    b.

    c.

9. Did the fact that God had promised it mean he did not have any responsibility to take it?

What lessons are in this for us?

10. How did he obtain help to take Debir?

What lessons do you see in this for those who are aging?

11. What was Caleb's "different spirit?" (See Deuteronomy 1:36)

How can we have such a "different spirit?"

12. What are some "mountains" we may face as we age?

13. When is a person "too old" to claim any promise God has made?

Chapter 6

Naomi

"Your daughter-in-law, who loves you…is better to you than seven sons" (Ruth 4:15).

Mother-in-law jokes abound in current conversation. Usually, the joke involves the mother-in-law of males. Studies, however, show that greater tensions are likely to develop between mothers-in-law and daughters-in-law. In a Time Magazine article, Jumana Farouky reports the result of one such study:

> In [a] book What Do You Want from Me? (out in the U.S. July 2009 and later in the U.K.), Terri Apter, a psychologist at Cambridge University, uses research gathered over the past 20 years to show that the relationship between female in-laws can be far more tense than the one between a man and his wife's mom. After speaking with 163 people, Apter discovered that more than 60% of women felt that friction with their husband's mother had caused them long-term stress…. In Apter's study, two-thirds of women said they felt their mothers-in-law were jealous of their relationships with the sons, while two-thirds of mothers-in-law said they felt excluded by their sons' wives.

In the Bible, we read of a woman and her daughter-in-law whose loving relationship was a blessing to both. If the story of Naomi and Ruth is not familiar to our readers, we recommend that before reading further, they take the few minutes needed to read the very short book called Ruth in the Old Testament. It will be a rewarding exercise, for the story is itself a literary classic.

The meaning of names is important in the book of Ruth as in much of the Old Testament. H.D.M. Spence in Pulpit Commentary says that the name Naomi means "God is sweet." Others say it means "pleasant". But during the years covered by the book, Naomi did not feel pleasant. In fact, she chose for herself the name Mara which means "bitter".

Mara

What made her life bitter?

First, a severe famine forced her and her family to leave their home in Bethlehem to migrate to Moab. Leaving one's home and attempting to adjust to the conditions in a foreign land may well induce bitterness. The idolatry of Moab would be a special irritant to one so pious as Naomi.

Next, she lost her husband and became a widow. Widows in those days were especially vulnerable, but at least she had her two sons to support her.

But her sons also died, leaving her with no source of support. She was desolate, a "widow indeed" as described in the New Testament (1 Timothy 5). Many who have experienced it tell us that the loss of a child is more devastating than the loss of a spouse. It is just not natural that children should go before their parents.

Furthermore, she fell victim to the same error as Job's friends: the notion that any calamity is a punishment by God for some sin. Note her explanation for her suffering: "the Lord has testified against me, and the Almighty has afflicted me" (1:21).

Finally, imagine how she felt when she returned to Bethlehem and friends who met her were startled by the change in her appearance. They asked, "Is this Naomi?" It was at this point that "she said to them, "Do not call me Naomi; call me Mara, for the Almighty has dealt very bitterly with me. I went out full, and the Lord has brought me home again empty" (1:20).

But though she felt that a name meaning "bitter" was more appropriate, it is evident that she was not a bitter old lady. People do not love and cling to bitter people as her son's widowed wives clung to her.

Qualities of Naomi

Unselfishness leads the list of good qualities she possessed. She could have insisted that her daughters-in-law go with her. "Who will take care of me?" she could have pled. Instead, she urged them not to go, believing that going would not be to their advantage. She was too old to bear sons for them to marry and they could better provide for themselves in their own homeland. Even when Ruth returned with her, her concern continued to be for Ruth's welfare, more than for her own.

Her godly character is evident. As a Jewess, her life so adorned the true religion that Ruth was not only attracted to Naomi but also to Naomi's people and to her God.

> Your people shall be my people,
> And your God, my God (1:16)

The arrangements Naomi made to encourage Boaz to marry Ruth were dictated by her knowledge of God's law and its provisions for widows.

Her wisdom is evident in the advice she gave day by day as Ruth went to glean in the fields. Even her scheme to gain Boaz as a husband for Ruth required considerable astuteness and skillful planning.

Naomi evidently spoke well of her daughter-in-law. When Ruth asked Boaz why he had been so kind to her,

> Boaz answered and said to her, "It has been fully reported to me, all that you have done for your mother-in-law since the death of your husband, and how you have left your father and your mother and the land of your birth, and

have come to a people whom you did not know before"
(2:11).

Where could this report have originated except with Naomi?

Much credit is also due to Ruth. Ruth was a loving daughter-
in-law, clinging to Naomi even when Orpah turned back.
Her respect for Naomi's advice is obvious as she followed it
to the letter. Even her generosity in sharing the results of her
gleaning is commendable. Yet, all of this is also a tribute to
Naomi who treated her, not as a daughter-in-law with whom
to compete but as a daughter to be loved and assisted. In fact,
Naomi calls Ruth her "daughter" at least five times in this
short story. This is a key to good relations.

Naomi's Reward

When Naomi's "daughter" had a baby, Naomi was a
grandmother! "Then Naomi took the child and laid him on
her bosom, and became a nurse to him" (4:16). "No one can
adequately put into words what occurs when a grandmother
magnetizes the heart of her youngest grandchild and they
share a moment that locks itself into eternity." (Johnnie
Godwin in *How to Retire Without Retreating*).

"Also the neighbor women gave him a name, saying, 'There is a son
born to Naomi'" (4:17). Because of that son, her name goes down
in history; that little "son" was the grandfather of the illustrious
King David. And who knows what good influence may have
trickled down through the generations to make David what he was?

No longer was she a desolate widow. Indeed, the women of the town said, "your daughter-in-law, who loves you,…is better to you than seven sons" (4:15).

Once again, she was Naomi! And all because she was a good mother-in-law. Indeed, "God is sweet."

Being Good In-laws

When a man and woman marry, there are many adjustments to be made. Few are more important than the forming of good relations with in-laws.

The bride must remember that the groom's mother has given him life and has nurtured him through many a crisis. He is what he is due, in part, to the love she has had for him and the care she has given him. She should not now be shut out of his life. She deserves continuing love and respect and a reasonable amount of time from a loving son. Even if she seems to desire more than is reasonable, the bride should try to be understanding.

At the same time, the mother of the groom needs to understand that he is now a man whose first duty is to his wife. God Himself decreed that "a man shall leave his father and mother and be joined to his wife, and they shall become one flesh" (Genesis 1:27). Her future happiness is most likely to be gained, not by grieving over the loss of a son, but by rejoicing that she now has gained a daughter to be loved. Once she develops true love for that daughter-in-law, she will

desire her happiness more than her own. "Love suffers long
and is kind; love does not envy; love does not parade itself, is
not puffed up; does not behave rudely, does not seek its own,
is not provoked, thinks no evil" (1 Corinthians 13:4-6).

If a little one is born, there will be no competition for
affection.

What is said here regarding mothers-in-law applies also to
fathers-in-law. The degree to which we love our children can
be measured by our desire for their happiness. We want their
married lives to be as peaceable and loving as possible, and
we are ready to contribute to their happiness, whether by
making ourselves accessible or by allowing some distance to
be maintained. It is their happiness we seek, not our own.

The result of such a relationship will often be as it was with
Ruth and Naomi. A daughter-in-law may indeed be better
to her mother-in-law than seven sons know how to be. How
often we have seen this among our acquaintances. One couple
reports relations so good that if they should ever break up, he
would have to go to her parents and she to his.

Being Good Grandparents

Solomon wrote, "Grandchildren are the crown of old men"
(Proverbs 17:6). One of the blessings offered to those who
fear the Lord: "You may see your children's children" (Psalm
126:6).

Each time a new grandchild is born, however there is a reminder of the seriousness of being a grandparent. At least three times in the Scriptures there is a warning to the effect that God "will by no means clear the guilty, visiting the iniquity of the fathers upon the children and the children's children to the third and the fourth generation" (Exodus 34:7). This does not mean that my descendants are guilty of my sins. Nor does it mean that God will single them out for punishment. It is simply that sin is so terrible that its consequences will trickle down to children and grandchildren. In some instances it may be disease that is passed down, or poverty or shame. Or it may be that my own weakness of character will keep me from teaching my children as they should be taught, with the effect that my grandchildren will also suffer a lack of knowledgeable and disciplined parents.

However it is, I will not suffer alone for my sins, Surely this is a sobering thought which should affect the choices of any loving parent or grandparent.

Thankfully, there is another side of the coin. "Therefore, know that the Lord your God, He is God, the faithful God who keeps covenant and mercy for a thousand generations with those who love Him and keep His commandments" (Deuteronomy 7:9). This means that the influence of a good life will trickle down in blessings to a thousand generations. I can be a light in the lives of my children and grandchildren long after I am gone. Even though King Josiah represented the 13th generation from David, it was said of him that "he did right in the Lord, and walked in the ways of his father, David" (2 Chronicles 34:2).

While we can only conjecture concerning Naomi's influence in David's life, there is no question about the influence of biblical Lois in the life of her grandson Timothy. Paul wrote to him, "I thank God…when I call to remembrance the genuine faith that is in you, which dwelt first in your grandmother Lois and your mother Eunice, and I am persuaded is in you also" (2 Timothy 1:3,5). This must explain the fact that Paul could write later: "From childhood you have known the Holy Scriptures, which are able to make you wise for salvation through faith which is in Christ Jesus" (2 Timothy 3:15). Timothy's father was an unbeliever, but this handicap was overcome by the influence of his mother and grandmother.

Years ago a young man who was not yet a Christian, came to our city to study art. Though surrounded by negative influences, there was one influence in his life that made the difference. A devout grandmother continued by long distance to encourage his obedience to the gospel. When he agreed, she called David Tant to baptize him. A weekly Bible study followed in his dormitory room and brethren provided transportation to services. When his faith grew weak, his grandmother stayed after him until he returned to the Lord. He became notably faithful, not only attending services but participating in frequent Bible classes, both as student and as teacher. He returned to his hometown to live with his grandmother, caring for her until she moved into an assisted living facility. He credits his grandmother as the channel through whom God changed his life.

Grandfathers can also serve. We recently attended a memorial service for a grandfather. Several of the grandchildren spoke for a few minutes. Each one, without exception, referred to the letters their grandfather had written them, some of the letters rebuking, some encouraging and all of them expressing a love that will go with them for the rest of their lives. "He, being dead, yet speaks."

Many of us have been influenced for good by ancestors whom we could not even name, as well as by those we have known. I have stood by the humble tombstones of my forefathers who were in Christ and thanked God for what they were. Our grandchildren are surrounded by constant negative influences and need every possible encouragement toward godliness. Let us, as grandparents, do what we can to supply that encouragement.

"Many daughters have done well, But you excel them all."
Charm is deceitful and beauty is passing, But a woman who fears the Lord, she shall be praised (Proverbs 31:29-30).

Memory Work

Fill in the blanks from memory:

Therefore we do not lose heart. Even though our _____
_ man is _____, yet the _____ man is being
_____ day by day. For our _____ affliction,
which is but for a moment, is working for us a far more
exceeding and eternal _____ of glory, while we do

not look at the things which are seen, but at the things which are not seen. For the things which are seen are ____ _____, but the things which are not seen are _____ _____ (2 Corinthians 4:16-18).

Questions

1. Do you agree that tensions are more common between mothers-in-law and their daughters-in-law than between them and their sons-in-law?

2. What are some definitions of the name, Naomi? What is the definition of the name Mara?

3. What were some circumstances Naomi faced that could easily make anyone bitter?

    a.

    b.

    c.

    d.

4. Why do you think Naomi encouraged her daughters-in-law not to go to Israel with her?

5. What lesson should mothers-in-law learn from Genesis 2:24?

6. What qualities in Naomi would encourage Ruth to insist on staying with her?

7. What evidence do you see of Naomi's godly character?

8. What demonstrates Naomi's wisdom?

9. Was Ruth's reputation helped or hindered by Naomi's conversations about her?

10. What does Naomi call Ruth in 3:1?

11. What is said of Ruth in 4:15?

12. Was it Naomi's fault that Orpah did not choose to go with her to Israel?   What does this say about the responsibility of daughters-in-law?

13. Why was Naomi able to fill the role of grandmother? Do you think she considered this full reward for all the kindness she had shown to Ruth?

14. Name some grandparents in the scriptures who influenced their grandchildren:

   a. For evil

   b. For good

16. Among your acquaintances, can you think of someone

who has been influenced for good by grandmothers or grandfathers?

16. What of your own faith? Has it been influenced by a good grandfather or grandmother?

17. What are some things grandparents can do to encourage godliness in their grandchildren?

Chapter 7

David

"The lamp of Israel" (2 Samuel 21:17).

As we grow older, numerous frustrations develop. Among these are:

• Having to discontinue some things we did well and took pride in doing.

• Being unable to reach goals we had hoped to reach.

• Suffering sickness that interferes with important responsibilities.

King David, though honored as a man after God's own heart, still experienced these things. We can learn from him how to deal with them.

Discontinuing What We Have Done Well

David made his name as a warrior. He first came to the attention of the general public when he killed the giant, Goliath. Almost immediately, he became a folk hero celebrated in song. "So, the women sang as they danced, and said:

> "Saul has slain his thousands, And David his ten thousands" (1 Samuel 18:7).

Under his leadership, the armies of Israel extended the borders of that nation to the greatest limits of its entire history. His counselor, Hushai, described him as "a man of war" (2 Samuel 18:7).

Yet, as David grew older, he experienced faintness in a battle with another giant and he had to be rescued by his nephew. "Then the men of David swore to him, saying, "You shall go out no more with us to battle, lest you quench the lamp of Israel" (2 Samuel 21:17).

It is often difficult for those of us who are older to give up activities in which we have taken some pride. "It's who I am," we say. Yet, it is often true that we can serve the Lord more effectively in some other way. God's glory must be our goal, not our own. David's role as "the lamp of Israel" was not as a warrior but as a prophet of God. The prophets Elijah and Elisha were never warriors, yet their godly influence qualified them as "the chariots of Israel and their horsemen" (2 Kings 2:12; 13:14).

David was blest to have advisors who were likely more objective in their assessments of his talents than he could be. There is no evidence that David resisted this call for retirement from warfare. If he had insisted on continuing to go to battle, he might well have been killed, making impossible the later achievements of his reign.

Gospel preachers sometimes promise God that they will preach till they die, and they insist on preaching even after they have lost their effectiveness. Elders, Bible teachers and song leaders can make the same mistake, often to the detriment of the cause they have served all their lives. The welfare of a congregation is much more important than fulfilling some personal commitment, regardless of how well intentioned it may have been. It is good to have family members who will advise us when it is time to give up. Under those circumstances, we will accomplish more good by humbly accepting their advice than by proudly insisting on continuing what we have been doing. One lesson we all must learn as we grow older: "To everything there is a season, A time for every purpose under heaven….I have seen the God-given task with which the sons of men are to be occupied. He has made everything beautiful in its time" (Ecclesiastes 3:1, 9-10). Contentment is possible when we are wise enough not to try to extend any activity beyond its time.

Failing to Reach a Noble Goal

David's early reign was imminently successful. Tribute poured in from conquered lands and he was able to build himself an expensive and beautiful palace, fit for the king that he had become. It troubled him, however, that while he lived in such luxury, the ark that represented the presence of God resided in a tent. He conceived the idea of a palace for God—a great temple. Nathan, the prophet of God, was favorably impressed with this plan and expressed his confidence that God, too, would approve.

But what seems good to men may not be what God desires (Proverbs 14:12; Isaiah 55:8-9). Even Nathan was wrong in his assessment. God asked Nathan,

> Wherever I have moved about with all the children of Israel, have I ever spoken a word to anyone from the tribes of Israel, whom I commanded to shepherd My people Israel, saying, "Why have you not built Me a house of cedar?" (2 Samuel 7:7).

This should be a lesson for all of us: that God will let us know what He desires, and it is presumptuous for us to try to guess about it. God desired a temple, but David was not the one to build it. To David, God said, "No."

What was David to do? Once he learned that God desired his son, Solomon, to build it (2 Samuel 7:12-13), he set out to assist that son in every way possible. He gave Solomon the plans for the building (1 Chronicles 28:11-12). He set aside huge amounts of very expensive materials to be used in construction (1 Chronicles 29:1-2). He encouraged others to contribute generously (1 Chronicles 29:5). And he prayed for the success of the project (1 Chronicles 29:10-20).

Often the plans we form for serving the Lord seem ideal to us. Yet, we may find ourselves thwarted in the fulfillment of those plans. If we are certain that it is a work approved by God, rather than being discouraged that we cannot do it, we need to look for ways to help others do it.

Harry Rimmer's books on evidences were among the most useful possessed by a past generation. But writing books on evidences was not his first choice for a life's work. In his book entitled *The Prayer Perfect*, he recalls that his first goal was to serve as a missionary in Africa.

> I did not stand quietly waiting for the door to open. I spent those seven years leaning on the door so that if it did open, I would fall through and be half way to Africa before anyone could shut it again! Surveying my present ministry, and in the light of the development of my own personal experience, I can see now that it would have been a mean trick on Africa if the Lord had allowed me to go. Instead, He has found for me a small place in the scheme of the kingdom, which I am filling, by His grace, to the best of my ability. In the intervening years, however, I have never lost my interest in foreign missions. It is a deep and constant comfort to my heart mentally to call the roll of those of my converts and students who are serving Christ on the foreign field today. Any one of them is doing more for missions than I ever could have done. (p.60).

Many of us, perhaps, have shared some of Rimmer's experiences. I can recall in my own life, a number of times when I felt some work would be exactly what God would want me to do, only to have what appeared to be an opportunity snatched from me. I have never quite understood why the apostle James was not allowed, because of his early martyrdom (Acts 12), to serve for as long as the other apostles, but God had His own agenda. Surely, it is for us to fit into His agenda as best we can without murmuring. If we are denied some opportunity which seems promising, we need simply to seek other ways to serve.

Suffering Sickness that Hinders

David had many sons. But God had revealed to David that Solomon, though not the eldest, should succeed him as King (1 Chronicles 28:5). It was David's responsibility to see that God's will was done.

But David was sick.

"Now King David was old, advanced in years; and they put covers on him, but he could not get warm" (1 Kings 1:1). David's eldest living son, Adonijah, took advantage of the situation to gather some influential men around him and arrange a coronation ceremony for himself. Nathan the prophet, who knew of God's choice, arranged to have David made aware of the situation.

What was David to do? In his weakened condition, he could well have said, "I'm just too old and too weak to do anything about this. It's God's choice. Maybe He will work it out somehow." Those who have been as old and ill as David was would surely understand. But this would not be the David of the Bible.

One can almost see a light come into the eyes of David. Sick or not sick, weak or strong, God's will had to be done. David went into action. "Call to me Zadok the priest, Nathan the prophet, and Benaiah the son of Jehoiada." So, they came before the king. The king also said to them,

> Take with you the servants of your Lord, and have Solomon my son ride on my own mule, and take him down to Gihon. There let Zadok the priest and Nathan the prophet anoint him king over Israel; and blow the horn, and say, 'Long live King Solomon!' Then you shall come up after him, and he shall come and sit on my throne, and he shall be king in my place. For I have appointed him to be ruler over Israel and Judah (1 Kings 1:32-35).

David found the strength to give Solomon a solemn charge:

> I go the way of all the earth; be strong, therefore, and prove yourself a man. And keep the charge of the Lord your God: to walk in His ways, to keep His statutes, His commandments, His judgments, and His testimonies, as it is written in the Law of Moses, that you may prosper in all that you do and wherever you turn (1 Kings 2:2-3).

The chronology is not certain, but it would also seem from First Chronicles 28 and 29 that David found the strength to call an assembly of Israel to confirm the choice of Solomon as king and to encourage construction of the temple.

I once knew an elder of the church who had served faithfully as a shepherd of the Lord's sheep. He found himself so enfeebled in his last days that he could not attend services. Still concerned for the sheep, he spent Sunday mornings on the phone during the worship hours, calling members of the church. Those who answered were prayed for if they were sick, but admonished if they were missing without cause.

Jesus, even in what we would call middle age, was in position to see the end of his life fast approaching. Preparing to heal a blind man, He said, "I must work the works of Him who sent Me while it is day; the night is coming when no one can work. As long as I am in the world, I am the light of the world" (John 9:4-5). Regardless of how old we may be, as long as we are in the world, we must let our light "so shine before men, that they may see [our] good works and glorify [our] Father in heaven" (Matthew 5:16).

Paul Earnhart, still preaching effectively in his late 80's, said it this way in a sermon in Garland, Texas:

> It is a serious loss to God's divine purpose when older saints grow dormant. The last of life is valuable too. There is no retirement from serving Christ; no furlough from God's army; no leave from our post. To take a permanent vacation on the lake or in the motor home (emphasis permanent) is not acceptable. This is not a time when we walk away from the kingdom of God to enjoy ourselves because we're free from some of the constraints and restrictions we knew at one time. No! It must go on. And

I'm saying to all my peers here this evening, "You are important to the task that God is intending us to carry. You are important to the working out of God's eternal purpose and when you fail to act in that area because you have decided that you're worthless, then that's a serious cost to the kingdom." So our older years are too valuable solely to spend them on things that do not influence eternity.

Paul Williams, at age 89, with macular degeneration in his eyes, hearing aids in his ears, and bereaved of his wife, continues to preach and work for the Lord in South Africa where he has served for 50 years. Wayne Partain, at age 93, continues to carry out a remarkable load of preaching, teaching and correspondence in Spanish.

Morituri Salutamus

What then? Shall we sit idly down and say
The night hath come; it is no longer day?
The night hath not yet come; we are not quite
Cut off from labor by the failing light;
Something remains for us to do or dare;
Even the oldest tree some fruit may bear;. . .
For age is opportunity no less
Than youth itself, though in another dress,
And as the evening twilight fades away
The sky is filled with stars, invisible by day.

— Henry Wadsworth Longfellow

Memory Work

Fill in the blanks from memory:

Therefore we do not lose heart. Even though our _____ man is _____, yet the _____man is being _____ _____ day by day. For our _____ affliction, which is but for a _____, is working for us a far more exceeding and _____ _____ of glory, while we do not look at the things which are seen, but at the things which are not seen. For the things which are seen are _____, but the things which are not seen are _____ (2 Corinthians 4:16-18).

Questions

1. For what was David most noted in his early years?

2. From what did he have to be rescued in 2 Samuel 21:15-17?

3. What did his men then insist that he do (or not do)?

4. Did this mean that he was no longer useful in Israel?

5. Have you ever known of anyone who insisted on continuing with a duty for which he was no longer qualified?

6. What lessons are here for us when we cannot do things we were once able to do effectively?

7. Does David's desire to build a temple for God seem

commendable? How did Nathan the prophet respond?

8. How did God respond? What lesson can we learn from this?

9. How did David help Solomon when God chose him rather than David to build the temple?

    a.

    b.

    c.

    d.

10. What was David's condition when it appeared that God's choice of his successor might be superseded by his brother?

11. How did David respond?

12. What are some things we can do for God, even as we see death approaching?

13. At what point in our physical decline do we cease to be responsible for doing God's will?

> *I will sing to the Lord as long as I live;*
> *I will sing praise to my God while I have my being.*

Psalm 104:33

Extra Thoughts

Another significant event in the life of David is recorded in 2 Samuel 24. It has not been included in this study because it is uncertain at what point in his life it occurred. It does seem probable that it was near the end of his life.

David ordered a census which was displeasing to God. It seems likely that it was motivated by pride in his victories and the size of his army. There is evidence that this pride was shared by the entire nation. and 70,000 of the people died in a plague that followed.

How may pride be a temptation to those who are aging?

Chapter 8

Barzillai

"Godliness with contentment is great gain." (1 Timothy 6:6)

I t is almost inevitable that money will become a matter of greater concern as we approach the time when we can no longer earn it.

Those of modest means practice frugality out of fear that they will not have enough to last the remainder of their lives. Others who have accumulated sufficient wealth to last several lifetimes have attained it by a similar frugality, and that habit does not change. Such frugality, whether among the rich or poor, can easily become stinginess.

Among the aged, however, you will also find some of the most generous people you will ever meet. Such a man was Barzillai at the age of eighty.

Barzillai's Generosity

David was on the run, fleeing with his followers from his son, Absalom. They had left Jerusalem in too much haste to gather the supplies they would desperately need. As they crossed the

Jordan, they were beyond the most likely sources of help. It was at this point that Barzillai came to their rescue.

> Barzillai the Gileadite from Rogelim, brought beds and basins, earthen vessels and wheat, barley and flour, parched grain and beans, lentils and parched seeds, honey and curds, sheep and cheese of the herd, for David and the people who were with him to eat. For they said, "The people are hungry and weary and thirsty in the wilderness" (2 Samuel 17:27-29).

When a person looks for reasons not to assist another in need, excuses can always be found. Barzillai could have given many reasons for refusing to help David. This was a war between David and his son; what reason did he have to be involved? What had David done for him to deserve assistance? What if Absalom was victorious and Barzillai had to face the consequences of helping David? Furthermore, he would be robbing his heirs if he gave so much to David.

Unlike Nabal (1 Samuel 25), however, Barzillai was not looking for excuses to refuse help, but for opportunities to extend it. In fact, he did not even wait to be asked. His generosity has earned him a favorable niche in scripture's hall of fame. An even greater reward is promised by David's illustrious descendant to those who exercise compassion toward His servants when they are in need.

> "When the Son of Man comes in His glory, and all the holy angels with Him, then He will sit on the throne of

His glory. All the nations will be gathered before Him, and He will separate them one from another, as a shepherd divides his sheep from the goats. And He will set the sheep on His right hand, but the goats on the left. Then the King will say to those on His right hand, "Come, you blessed of My Father, inherit the kingdom prepared for you from the foundation of the world: for I was hungry and you gave Me food; I was thirsty and you gave Me drink; I was a stranger and you took Me in; I was naked and you clothed Me; I was sick and you visited Me; I was in prison and you came to Me."… And the King will answer and say to them, "Assuredly, I say to you, inasmuch as you did it to one of the least of these My brethren, you did it to Me" (Matthew 25:31-40).

Barzillai's Contentment

David was exceedingly grateful for Barzillai's assistance and undertook to reward him. Following the defeat of Absalom, David was called to return to his throne in Jerusalem. As he began his triumphant homecoming, various ones came to accompany him.

And Barzillai the Gileadite came down from Rogelim and went across the Jordan with the king, to escort him across the Jordan. Now Barzillai was a very aged man, eighty years old. And he had provided the king with supplies while he stayed at Mahanaim, for he was a very rich man. And the king said to Barzillai, "Come across with me, and I will provide for you while you are with me in Jerusalem." "But Barzillai said to the king, "How long have I to live, that I should go up with the king to Jerusalem? I am today eighty years old. Can I discern between the good and bad? Can your servant taste what I eat or what I drink? Can I hear any longer the voice of singing men and singing women? Why then should your servant be a further burden to my lord the king? Your servant will go a little way across the Jordan with the king. And why should the king repay me with such a reward? Please let your servant turn back again, that I may die in my own city, near the grave of my father and mother. But here is your servant Chimham; let him cross over with my lord the king, and do for him what seems good to you (2 Samuel 19:31-37).

Eighty years old, nearing death, discernment fading, taste lost, hearing failing. Many a man in that condition is bitter and cranky, consumed only with his own handicaps. Not Barzillai. There was a becoming contentment shining from within the feeble body of that aged saint. The recital of his handicaps was not a complaint but an explanation for not accepting the gracious invitation extended by David. He was sufficiently grateful for what he had that he did not covet more.

C. Chapman in *Pulpit Commentary*, (Vol. 4, p. 478) makes these observations, based on the few verses that describe him.

In Barzillai we see all the natural, physical beauties of age crowned by virtues of the most unusual kind. His generous

provision for the king when in need, and his making
an effort to see him happily on his way home, revealed
kindliness. His desire to share in such valued society
so far as strength permitted, his right estimate of what
befits the closing days of life, and his quiet content with
the comforts and joys of home, show his *wisdom.* His
anxiety not to be a burden to the king amidst the duties
and cares of government, and his request for a favor
to his son (1 Kings 2:7), prove his *considerateness.* His
wish to live and die and be buried among the kindred
whom he had loved so long, was evidence of his *domestic
affection.* His having befriended, honored, and loved
the banished king when appearances were against him,
and his being privileged to take so tender a leave of the
Lord's anointed, was a sign of distinguished loyalty. His
obvious faith in the right cause when the rebellion was
at its height, his bold identification of his interests with
those of the Lord's affected servant, his doing all for the
right cause without any idea of compensation, was proof
of deep *piety.*

Thus, the beauty of old age lies much in years being
crowned with kindliness of disposition, wisdom of
conduct, consideration of feeling, deep affection for
ones own people, faithfulness in the relations of life, and
calm and strong piety. How lovely is old age when so
adorned!

That's the kind of old man I want to be.

Practicing Generosity

In our desire to be generous like Barzillai, conscientious seniors face some serious problems. Surely it is right for us to do what we can to provide for our own future needs; we want to avoid being a burden on others. In fact, Paul quotes with approval what appears to have been an accepted axiom of his day: "Children ought not to lay up for the parents, but the parents for the children" (2 Corinthians 12:14). Solomon observed, "A good man leaves an inheritance to his children's children" (Proverbs 13:22). Should we jeopardize our own security and the inheritance of our children to give to others in need?

God does not ask others to do what Jesus asked the rich young ruler to do—to sell all he had to give to the poor. It is not wrong, even to be rich, so long as we maintain the qualities commended by the Holy Spirit.

> Command those who are rich in this present age not to be haughty, nor to trust in uncertain riches but in the living God, who gives us richly all things to enjoy. Let them do good, that they be rich in good works, ready to give, willing to share, storing up for themselves a good foundation for the time to come, that they may lay hold on eternal life (1 Timothy 6:17-19).

At the same time, the Spirit through John wrote, "Whoever has this world's goods, and sees his brother in need, and shuts up his heart from him, how does the love of God abide in him" (1 John 3:17). When Paul was raising funds for the poor in Judea, he commended the generosity of the poor Macedonians.

> In a great trial of affliction the abundance of their joy and their deep poverty abounded in the riches of their liberality. For I bear witness that according to their ability, yes, and beyond their ability, they were freely willing" (2 Corinthians 8:2-3).

The fields that the brethren in Jerusalem sold for the relief of their fellow-disciples were very likely what they were depending on for their retirement.

How do we reconcile these two ideas: the need to save for future needs and yet, the need to give to the point of sacrificing our savings? Obviously, the needs in Jerusalem on at least those two occasions represented emergencies. Emergencies demand heroic responses, and brethren responded, even to the point of extraordinary sacrifice. Theirs was an act of faith, trusting God to provide for their future needs. The promises of such provisions abound in scripture. For example: "He who has pity on the poor lends to the Lord, and He will pay back what he has given" (Proverbs 19:17). And it is a fact that after brethren in Jerusalem gave away their retirement fund, their later needs were met by the Gentile churches in response to Paul's appeal. David observed, "I have been young, and now am old; yet I have not seen the righteous forsaken, nor his descendants begging bread" (Psalm 37:25).

In her book, *Talking with God in Old Age*, Missy Buchanan expresses the dilemma this way:

> When you don't know how long you'll live, it's hard not to care about money.
>
> Will I have enough to last me? That question never strays far from my mind.
>
> Some people think I'm a cheapskate. They snicker at my fuddy-duddy ways, like saving coupons and taking advantage of early-bird specials.
>
> They don't understand why I cringe at the prices of things. Just thinking about money eats away at my peace of mind.
>
> Sure, I'd like to be more generous, but how do I know what I can afford? The last thing I want to do is run out of money and become a burden to others.
>
> If only I knew how much longer I will live. That's the unknown in the math equation of life. Maybe I'll live five more years. Maybe fifteen. Or maybe I'll die tomorrow.
>
> Dear God, help me to be wise, but not obsessed with thriftiness. Help me to loosen my grip on money and grab hold of you instead. In the uncertainties of life, I will trust you. For the length of my life is an uncertain mystery. (pp. 13,14)

Learning Contentment

Barzillai's contentment, even in his infirmities, is notable. Yes, he was rich. But contentment is never traceable to one's financial status. If anything, discontent seems to be more often the failing of the wealthy than of the poor. Contentment is not the product of external conditions, but of internal qualities. Someone has said that contentment is not having all you want but wanting all you have.

Gratitude is the mother of contentment.

This is clearly seen in the Apostle Paul as he thanked the Philippians for a gift they had sent. He writes,

> Not that I speak in regard to need, for I have learned in whatever state I am, to be content: I know how to be abased, and I know how to abound. Everywhere and in all things I have learned both to be full and to be hungry, both to abound and to suffer need. I can do all things through Christ who strengthens me (Philippians 4:11-13).

If Paul could "learn" it, we can learn it too, regardless of our surroundings.

A number of years ago when preaching overseas, we received a generous monthly check from a lady in Texas. It was some time before I learned how she was able to support our work. Late in life, she married a very wealthy man whose wife had died. When he passed away, he left most of what he had to his children. However, he provided for her to have a modest monthly income to cover expenses, he made certain that she was permitted to live in their fine residence until she died, and he willed her all its furnishings. She was grateful for his thoughtfulness, but it left her living in luxury while unable to give anything significant to the cause that meant so much to her. What could she do?

Then it occurred to her. She could sell the expensive furniture pieces that were hers and from the proceeds she could support evangelists. This is what she did for as long as the furniture lasted. She was a happy lady, content to rattle around in a mansion, almost empty of furniture, because her future needs were assured and, at the same time, she was able to contribute significantly to the Lord's work.

> "So teach us to number our days,
> That we may gain a heart of wisdom."
> Psalm 90:12

Memory Work

Fill in the blanks from memory:

> Therefore we do not lose heart. Even though our _____
> __ man is _____, yet the _____ man is being
> _____ day by day. For our _____ affliction,
> which is but for a _____, is working for us a far more

exceeding and _____ _____ of glory, while
we do not look at the things which are _____, but at the
things which are not _____. For the things which are
seen are _____, but the things which are not seen
are _____. (2 Corinthians 4:16-18)

Questions

1. How old was Barzillai?

2. What was his physical condition?

3. List some of the qualities he possessed.

4. What were some reasons he could have given for avoiding
any involvement with David?

    a.

    b

    c.

5. Read the story of Nabal in 1Samuel 25 and contrast him
with Barzillai.

6. When we see someone in need do we look for excuses not
to help or for opportunities to do so?

7. In the judgment scene of Matthew 25:31-46

a. What is the basis for reward or rejection?

b. Who represents Christ when we help or reject them (verses 40,45)?

c. Does this eliminate others who may be in need (Galatians 6:10)?

8. Is it sinful to be rich? (See 1 Timothy 6:17-19) Note: Most of us are rich compared to a majority of the world's population.

a, What are the dangers of being rich?

b. How does God want us to feel about his generous gifts to us (verse 17)?

c. What responsibilities do rich people have?

d. What are they doing as they share their wealth (verse 19)?

9. How can we balance the need to be generous against the need to avoid being a burden on others in our later years?

10. What promises do the scriptures contain for those who are generous in giving?

11. What are some externals as we age that give an excuse for discontent?

12. How can we learn contentment, even in the face of such external conditions?

Chapter 9

Jeremiah

"Yet they did not obey or incline their ear" (Jer. 11:8).

The fear of irrelevance is common for those who are aging. In our western culture, this is increasingly real for seniors. "The world has passed us by. We are out of touch with what is going on around us. No one listens to us anymore." A ninety year old lady was heard to remark that she did not bother to think any more. When asked why, she said, "Nobody cares what I think."

Older people are all too often placed in isolation where they will not be a bother to anyone. The time may not be too far in the future when the same philosophy that allows for the killing of unwanted newborns may justify the killing of unwanted and irrelevant old folks.

In primitive cultures, age is still equated with wisdom. Those who are older have experienced most of what is to be experienced, and what they have not experienced they have observed. They know what works and what doesn't work. They have seen the consequences of good and evil. Job expressed this concept. "Wisdom is with aged men, and with length of days, understanding" (Job 12:12).

In western culture, however, wisdom is not measured by age but by one's expertise in the use of technology. Children are proficient with technology that did not even exist in the earlier lifetime of the aged. Grandpa and Grandma are so dumb about cell phones and computers, and it is easy to assume that they are dumb about everything else. "They just don't get it!" What too many young people do not understand, however, is that the aged may very well "get it" when it comes to the things that really matter for truly successful living. True happiness is not produced by gadgets.

Disregard for the counsel of the aged is not new. Examples of it are found in scripture. Elihu, the younger of Job's friends, expressed his skepticism: "Great men are not always wise, nor do the aged always understand justice" (Job 32:9). And there are other examples of this as well.

Rehoboam's Counselors

King Solomon was a great builder, but it was at the expense of his citizens. When he died, the people asked his successor, Rehoboam, for relief from the load they had carried.

> Then King Rehoboam consulted the elders who stood
> before his father Solomon while he still lived, and he said,
> "How do you advise me to answer these people?" And
> they spoke to him, saying, "If you will be a servant to

these people today, and serve them, and answer them, and speak good words to them, then they will be your servants forever." But he rejected the advice which the elders had given him, and consulted the young men who had grown up with him, who stood before him (1 Kings 13:6-8).

The young men advised him to increase the load, and Rehoboam followed their counsel to his detriment. A rebellion broke out which cost him five-sixths of his kingdom. The "elders" were right.

Jeremiah

Jeremiah's counsel was rejected even when he was young. This was because he was not merely mouthing the wisdom of his peers, but revealing the wisdom of the "Ancient of Days", the God of Heaven, whose "age" is infinite. Because the wisdom of God, spoken by Jeremiah, did not agree with the wisdom of his time, the people rejected it. A king who read his warnings, took a pen knife and cut them up page by page and threw them into the fire (Jeremiah 36:20-26). God warned Jeremiah in advance that his people would not listen (Jeremiah 1:17-19).

Jeremiah may have hoped that as he grew older and his predictions came true one by one, the people would eventually listen. In his late sixties, the Babylonians surrounded Jerusalem, just as he had predicted, and their victory appeared imminent. King Zedekiah sent for him secretly, and Jeremiah must have thought that

at last his advice would be heeded. He advised Zedekiah
to surrender. The king seemed to see the wisdom of his
counsel, but he wavered as he sent Jeremiah on his way.
Just as always, Jeremiah's counsel was rejected, and the
king suffered the consequences. He was captured by the
Babylonians, his sons were slaughtered in his presence,
his eyes were then put out, and he was taken in chains to
Babylon.

When Jerusalem fell and the majority of its citizens were
deported, Jeremiah was given a choice of going or staying. He
chose to stay in the land with the few who remained. In the
turmoil that followed, out of fear of the Babylonians, a plan
was formed for the group to migrate to Egypt. But before the
decision was made, the leaders came to Jeremiah, asking him
to seek counsel from the Lord.

> They said to Jeremiah, "Let the Lord be a true and
> faithful witness between us, if we do not do according
> to everything which the Lord your God sends us by you.
> Whether it is pleasing or displeasing, we will obey the voice
> of the Lord our God to whom we send you, that it may be
> well with us when we obey the voice of the Lord our God"
> (Jeremiah 42:5-6).

Now at last he was to have some credibility. Maybe being seventy
had earned him the respect he should have had all along.

But alas, it was not to be. When he reported that the Lord
disapproved of their going, they responded, "You speak

falsely! The Lord our God has not sent you to say, 'Do not go to Egypt to dwell there'" (Jeremiah 43:2). Once more, younger people had rejected his advice, even though the counsel was from the Lord.

Continuing Without Compromise

When we are older and our counsel is rejected, four possibilities face us. One is to grow bitter and acrimonious. This totally destroys any hope we may have of influencing the rising generation; no one listens to a grouchy old man or woman.

Another possibility is to keep quiet and avoid confrontation of any kind.

The third is to compromise our convictions and accept the deviant beliefs and conduct of those who are younger in order to gain some honor from them. This is sometime approved as "mellowing."

The last is to lovingly insist that young people comply with what we believe to be right.

If our differences with youth are mere tradition or preference, we may well compromise or just remain quiet about our opinions. Neither tradition nor personal preference is important enough to justify the conflict and loss of influence that often follows. There is a wisdom, however, that we cannot compromise. It is not the wisdom produced by our experiences and observations, but the wisdom of God contained in scripture. Paul wrote,

> We speak wisdom among those who are mature, yet not the wisdom of this age, nor of the rulers of this age, who are coming to nothing. But we speak the wisdom of God in a mystery, the hidden wisdom which God ordained before the ages for our glory (1 Corinthians 2:6-7).

Jesus said that God's word is truth (John 17:17), and truth does not change with generations and cultures. "Speaking the truth in love" is always the ideal (Ephesians 4:15).

What a wonderful example Jeremiah is! He was tenderhearted and compassionate, earning a reputation as the "weeping prophet." His love could not be questioned. Yet, there was never a compromise of his message because it came from God. When God called him, he instructed him: "you shall go to all to whom I send you, and whatever I command you, you shall speak" (Jeremiah 1:7). This he did faithfully to the day he died, and this we must do to our own last day as well.

> Weeping may endure for a night,
> But joy comes in the morning.
> Psalm 30:5

Dealing with Relocation

When Jeremiah was taken to Egypt he was taken against his wishes. He even knew that God did not approve the move.

Today, older people sometimes suffer a similar fate.

Sometimes the aged are placed in nursing homes against their will. There are times when this is done for their benefit—their needs are beyond the ability of children to provide proper care. Sometimes, however, it is an unwillingness of family members to care for their own. Regardless of the reason, the Christian senior must make the best of the situation.

One Christian lady we knew voluntarily entered such a home in order to go through the rooms and read the Bible to those who would welcome her. Soon after entering an assisted living facility at the age of 99, Sam Binkley began studying the Bible with one of the employees. She was baptized soon after his 100th birthday and just two weeks before his death. Often arrangements can be made to bring in Christians from outside to conduct classes and even services.

Occasionally children, on whom parents must depend for support, move them to places where the Lord's church cannot be found or where transportation is not available.

God knows the true desires of the heart. "For if there is first a willing mind, it is accepted according to what one has, and not according to what he does not have" (2 Corinthians 8:12). John, the apostle, found himself exiled on the Isle of Patmos "on the Lord's Day," far removed from the assembly of the saints (Revelation 1:10). He reports that he was "in the Spirit." This we can be as well, even if we are not inspired by the Spirit as he was. The Lord's Day is a good time to spend in Bible reading, prayers and songs. Modern inventions such as radios, TV's, and computers make it possible to hear good teaching though we are confined. Many churches now stream their services. Listening to such streaming is not a substitute for assembling, but if it is all one can do it is far better than nothing and it is gratifying indeed to the deprived Christian.

Where there is a will, however, there is often a way. If the victim of such a move shows sufficient eagerness to worship with the saints, the opportunity may well be provided. Younger Christians can often be found who are willing to drive some distance out of their way to assist the elderly with transportation, especially if proper gratitude is expressed. Even without help, some heroic efforts have sometime been successful.

Eddie Mae Caldwell was a Christian widow living in West Tennessee. With no one there to care for her, it was necessary for her to move to Atlanta where her son lived. Not wanting to be in his way, however, she rented an apartment, carefully choosing one within walking distance of a church she had located. Immediately, she became an active part of the church, attending regularly and often bringing visitors. This ideal arrangement continued until circumstances changed and she had no choice but to move in with her son who lived twenty-five miles from the meeting place. What was she to do?

It was evident to anyone who had seen her driving cautiously along the city streets that she could not manage Atlanta interstates. We looked at maps to try to locate a closer congregation; we tried to find people living close enough to her son to provide transportation. But all to no avail. We bade her goodbye with much regret, wondering how she would cope and anticipating sadly the void there would be in our assembly the following Sunday.

Next Sunday, her little brown Chevette pulled in as usual, only a little earlier. Thinking she had not completed her move or had spent the night nearby, I asked, "How did you get here?"

"I drove," was the simple reply. And drive she did each Sunday until her health prevented.

A solution to the problem of isolation is not always possible, but every opportunity will be sought by those who truly desire to avoid "forsaking the assembly" (Hebrews 10:25).

> This is the day the Lord has made;,
> We will rejoice and be glad in it.
> Psalm 118:24

Memory Work

Fill in the blanks from memory:

Therefore we do not lose _____. Even though our
_____ man is _____, yet the _____
man is being _____ day by day. For our _____
affliction, which is but for a _____, is working for us a
far more _____ and _____ _____ of
glory, while we do not look at the things which are _____

but at the things which are not _____. For the things
which are seen are _____, but the things which are
not seen are _____ (2 Corinthians 4:16-18).

Questions

1. What are some reasons that the elderly are considered
irrelevant in western culture?

2. What are some mistakes the elderly can make that may
cause others to ignore them?

3. When Rehoboam sought advice, who was right, the young
counselors or the old?

4. Why was Jeremiah's message ignored, even when he was a
young man?

5. As aging Christians, we will often find ourselves in
disagreement with younger people about many things. What
things are not worth arguing about?

6. What are four possible reactions when young people reject
God's wisdom?

    a.

    b.

c.

d.

Which of these did Jeremiah choose?

7. What does Jeremiah's example teach us about the proper attitude in our controversies?

8. What are some things that may be forced upon us in our later years that we may not choose?

9. What are some things that can be done in a home for seniors to continue serving the Lord?

10. How can our attitude determine the assistance we are given?

11. What passage suggests that God does not expect more of us than we can do?

Chapter 10

Daniel

*"I, Daniel, understood by the books... Then I set my
face toward the Lord God" (Daniel 9:2-3).*

"Iron sharpens iron," the scriptures say. But as we age,
those thought-provoking conversations that helped
to mold us become less frequent. Our peers become
fewer, and younger people find curious the past about
which we like to reminisce. Old friends who do remain are
often inaccessible, thinking in a different channel, suffering
from dementia or deaf. These things make conversations
difficult. This is one of the burdens of aging.

As a young man, Daniel was captured with many of his Jewish
comrades and taken away to Babylon. He found himself
with three comrades chosen to serve in Nebuchadnezzar's
court. Many stimulating conversations must have taken place
between Daniel and his three friends as they found themselves
challenged by the requirements of the court (Daniel, chapter
one).

Again, in chapter two, they join him in prayer for wisdom to
interpret Nebuchadnezzar's dream. His friends appear again

in chapter three, but not with Daniel, and after this they disappear from the record. Indeed, we know nothing of any companions Daniel had in later years who shared his faith. But Daniel was not without conversation; he conversed with God.

If conversation is defined as an exchange of thoughts between two or more people, Daniel both listened and talked to God. True, he was a prophet through whom God spoke directly on special occasions. But Daniel did not depend on this. He recognized the written words of other prophets as messages from God. In his late eighties, he was reading those words and seeking to understand the message they contained. When he did understand, he applied them to his circumstances and responded by talking to God in prayer. All of this is clearly implied or stated in chapter nine of Daniel.

Listening to God

> In the first year of Darius the son of Ahasuerus, of the lineage of the Medes, who was made king over the realm of the Chaldeans—in the first year of his reign I, Daniel, understood by the books the number of the years specified by the word of the Lord through Jeremiah the prophet, that He would accomplish seventy years in the desolations of Jerusalem (Daniel 9:1-2).

Here, Daniel clearly states that he read the writings of Jeremiah in which Jeremiah predicted that the captivity of the Jews in Babylon would last for seventy years. He read them,

not as the word of Jeremiah but as "the word of the Lord
through Jeremiah." Later, in chapter 9:13, he reveals that he
read the Law of Moses, where the captivity had been foretold
by Moses nearly 1,000 years earlier.

But Daniel not only read these passages; he says he
understood them. He thought about them and reasoned from
them in order to understand his times and how he should
respond. He calculated the number of years that Jeremiah had
foretold and realized that the time had come for the end of
the captivity. He fully expected that release to occur, but on
the conditions that had been stated.

The conditions had been stated in "the Law of Moses" which
he had also read. In Leviticus 26, after predicting the scattering
of His people because of their disobedience, God promised:

> But if they confess their iniquity and the iniquity of their
> fathers, with their unfaithfulness in which they were
> unfaithful to Me, and that they also have walked contrary
> to Me, and that I also have walked contrary to them and
> have brought them into the land of their enemies; if their
> uncircumcised hearts are humbled, and they accept their
> guilt— then I will remember My covenant with Jacob, and
> My covenant with Isaac and My covenant with Abraham I
> will remember; I will remember the land (verses 40-42).

The conditions were clear. First, the guilt of the nation and
their fathers must be confessed. Second, the fact that their
captivity was God's punishment and that it was fully deserved

must be acknowledged. Finally, humility must be evident in their approach to God.

Now what does Daniel do? Knowing his history, it is not surprising to find him—

Talking to God

He was always a man of prayer. Even when threatened with the lion's den, "he went home. And in his upper room, with his windows open toward Jerusalem, he knelt down on his knees three times that day, and prayed and gave thanks before his God, as was his custom since early days" (Daniel 6:10). His opening his windows to pray toward Jerusalem implies that he had also read Solomon's prayer in 1 Kings 8:30. "And may You hear the supplication of Your servant and of Your people Israel, when they pray toward this place."

The prayer that Daniel offered has been a marvel of God's people through the ages. Without doubt, his meditation on the prediction of Jeremiah, the Law of Moses, and the prayer of Solomon contributed to the piety so beautifully reflected in his own prayer. He was responding to God.

Read the prayer recorded in Daniel 9:3-19. Notice first, that this was not one of his three times a day prayers; this one was a special one for which he prepared "with fasting, sackcloth, and ashes" (vs. 3). This suggests a dedicated time for special prayer. Note further how he included each of the elements Leviticus required.

Confession:

> I prayed to the Lord my God, and made confession, and
> said, 'O Lord… we have sinned and committed iniquity,
> we have done wickedly and rebelled, even by departing
> from Your precepts and Your judgments. Neither have we
> heeded Your servants the prophets…' (verses 4-6).

Later,

> To the Lord our God belong mercy and forgiveness,
> though we have rebelled against Him. We have not obeyed
> the voice of the Lord our God, to walk in His laws, which
> He set before us by His servants the prophets. Yes, all Israel
> has transgressed Your law, and has departed so as not to
> obey Your voice. (Verses 9-11a).

> "We have sinned, we have done wickedly" (verse 15)!

Acknowledgement of God as the source of their captivity.

> Therefore, the curse and the oath written in the Law
> of Moses the servant of God have been poured out on
> us, because we have sinned against Him. And He has
> confirmed His words, which He spoke against us and
> against our judges who judged us, by bringing upon us a
> great disaster; for under the whole heaven such has never
> been done as what has been done to Jerusalem. As it is
> written in the Law of Moses, all this disaster has come
> upon us; yet we have not made our prayer before the Lord

our God, that we might turn from our iniquities and understand Your truth. Therefore the Lord has kept the disaster in mind, and brought it upon us; for the Lord our God is righteous in all the works which He does, though we have not obeyed His voice (Verses 11b-14).

Humbled Hearts:

O Lord, righteousness belongs to You, but to us shame of face, as it is this day…O Lord, to us belongs shame of face, to our kings, our princes, and our fathers, because we have sinned against You (verses 7, 8).

O my God, incline Your ear and hear; open Your eyes and see our desolations, and the city which is called by Your name; for we do not present our supplications before You because of our righteous deeds, but because of Your great mercies (Verse 18).

This prayer of Daniel was acknowledged by God as the fulfillment of the conditions for return and an angel came to assure Daniel that his prayer was heard. Shortly after the prayer, Cyrus issued the decree that permitted the Jews to leave Babylon and return to their homeland. Daniel did not return (because of age?) but without doubt his prayer was instrumental in gaining the release of his people.

Truly, "The effective, fervent prayer of a righteous man avails much" (James 5:16). But the prayers of a truly righteous man will be seasoned with the wisdom of God that has been gained from sincere reading of His word with understanding and application.

Practical Application

For our senior years, the world offers numerous ways to spend our time. Many communities have Senior Centers where one may go, play games, eat and engage in other planned activities. We can travel, play golf, watch television, or just sleep the time away. Much of this is innocent but a relatively wasteful use of time. How much better to use more of it in study and prayer.

Actually, prayer is very popular with many in our day. In fact, it is more popular than Bible study. It is touted as a means of receiving messages from God through some other channel than His written word. A whole genre of books has appeared recently offering messages direct from God in response to prayer. It is true that a person can reach such an emotional high, expecting God to speak, that voices will be heard. These voices, however, come from one's own subconscious, not from God.

God has never communicated with His people in this way. Messages to people like Abraham came only occasionally. It was sometimes 25 years between God's direct messages to Abraham, and this was before His word was written. When God did communicate a message, it was usually to a prophet for publication to others or it was something essential to His purpose for all mankind.

We talk to God in prayer; God talks to us in the Bible.

Conversation is best between individuals who know each other well.

As our creator, of course, God knows us perfectly. This has made it possible for Him to inspire a message that is relevant to every human need.

> All Scripture is given by inspiration of God, and is profitable for doctrine, for reproof, for correction, for instruction in righteousness, that the man of God may be complete, thoroughly equipped for every good work (2 Timothy 3:16-17).

We know God in some measure through nature and the Old Testament. But it is in the New Testament, especially in the person of Jesus, that we come to know Him best. "No one has seen God at any time. The only begotten Son, who is in the bosom of the Father, He has declared Him" (John 1:18). Jesus said further, "He who has seen Me has seen the Father" (John 14:9).

Hearing God in the Bible, plus talking to Him in prayer is the conversation that can be so enriching *even in the absence of friends or acquaintances. Prayer without study is monologue, not dialogue.*

In his book, *The Joy of Growing Old in Christ,* Dee Bowman includes a chapter entitled, "The Joy of Knowing as You Age."

He writes:

> There is a certain thrill to learning—especially about
> learning new bits of information about things of interest to
> you. Newfound truths are exciting, no matter your age. The
> Scriptures are an inexhaustible well of learning. Its truth is
> never-ending; the joy of finding it never grows old. This joy
> is, in fact, magnified for those of us who are older. Why?
> Simple. We are closer to the end. New truths make our
> faith even stronger, make our hope more visible. (p. 47)

When we study God's word as Daniel did, we will be moved
to pray as Daniel prayed. God's word is a mirror in which we
see reflected, not only our own faults but the moral decline
of our nation and the depravity of the world around us. We
have a choice. We can become bitter and accusatory or, as
Daniel, we can talk to God about it, confess our own sins
and those of our people, humbly ask His forgiveness and seek
opportunities to wield a godly influence in the world before
we leave it. "Dare to be a Daniel."

Modern Examples

I think I have known some Daniels who choose to spend
increasing time in study as they age. I visited with Morris
Norman, after his preaching days were over, and found him
spending hours each day studying God's word, especially the
prophets. One brother I know, who is in his late eighties,
expresses thanks for his blindness, observing that it has forced
him to withdraw from his usual busy life and allowed him

to spend hours each day listening to recordings of God's word. Among other books that Homer Hailey wrote were a commentary on the book of Job written at the age of ninety-five and one on Daniel that was published after his death at the age of ninety-seven.

Are there those today who spend hours in prayer, preparing "with fasting, sackcloth, and ashes"? I don't know. Perhaps there are Christians who do so in their "secret place" where no one knows. I think it is likely. But thinking about Daniel gives me the motivation to increase my own time in prayer as well as in study, and I hope it may encourage others to do the same. God gives us the time, especially as we grow older. The question is, how do we use it?

Memory Work

Fill in the blanks from memory:

Therefore we do not lose _____. Even though our _____ man is _____, yet the _____ man is being _____ day by day. For our _____ affliction, which is but for a _____, is working for us a far more _____ and _____ _____ of glory, while we do not _____ at the things which are _____, but at the things which are not _____. For the things which are seen are _____, but the things which are not seen are _____. (2 Corinthians 4:16-18)

Questions

1. What are the benefits of deep conversations with godly companions? Can you give some examples from your own life's experiences?

2. What circumstances often limit the possibility of such conversations as we grow older?

3. Daniel read "the word of the Lord through Jeremiah, the prophet." How does belief in verbal inspiration heighten the sense of God's speaking to us?

4. How did God speak to "the fathers"? (Hebrews 1:1) How does He speak to us?

5. What passages teach that we do not need any communication from God other than what we receive from the scriptures?

6. What are some excuses we make for failing to spend time reading?

7, What are some other things we do that could be curtailed to make more time for reading?

8. Suggest some rules that help to establish good habits of bible reading.

9. What is needed beyond mere Bible reading?

10. What are some questions we should ask ourselves as we read?

11. How does time spent in the word prepare us for prayer?

12. Using Daniel's prayer as an example, what are some things that are proper in a prayer?

13. Are there times when prayer might well be accompanied with fasting? What does fasting involve? If one chooses to fast, is it something to be reported to others (See Matthew 6:16-18)?

14. Do you know any Christians who are good examples of Bible study and prayer?

15. What are some reactions to the moral decline in our nation that are worthless? What responses are approved (See 1 Timothy 2:1-4; Ephesians 5:11)?

Chapter 11

Simeon and Anna

"We have seen the Lord" John 20:25.

W hat do you dream of doing before you die? I knew a man many years ago whose stated goal was to accumulate a million dollars before he died. An early death prevented his reaching it. Others have hoped to visit some distant country, to climb some mountain or even to walk on the moon. We have seen the desire of Moses to enter the promised land. But Luke, chapter two, tells of an aged man who had a remarkable promise made to him by the Holy Spirit regarding his future. It was fulfilled when he held a baby, less than six weeks old, in his arms.

The baby had been born in Bethlehem, just six miles from where the old man lived. Now his parents had brought him to the temple in Jerusalem for the sacrifice of redemption required by the law. They knew the details of their baby's miraculous conception, and they could not forget the remarkable visit of the shepherds the night of His birth. The shepherds reported that angels had called Him "a Savior who is Christ the Lord." Now what might await them at the temple?

Simeon

And behold, there was a man in Jerusalem whose name was
Simeon, and this man was just and devout, waiting for the
Consolation of Israel, and the Holy Spirit was upon him.
And it had been revealed to him by the Holy Spirit that he
would not see death before he had seen the Lord's Christ.
So he came by the Spirit into the temple. And when
the parents brought in the Child Jesus, to do for Him
according to the custom of the law, he took Him up in his
arms and blessed God and said:

"Lord, now You are letting Your servant depart in peace,
According to Your word;
For my eyes have seen Your salvation Which You have
prepared before the face of all peoples,
A light to *bring* revelation to the Gentiles,
And the glory of Your people Israel."
And Joseph and His mother marveled at those things
which were spoken of Him (Luke 2:25-32).

Knowing what we know about the little one who was cradled
in the old man's arms, we might very well agree that it was the
experience of a lifetime. Who of us would not rejoice at such
a privilege?

But the fact is that ours is a privilege greater than that of
Simeon. Guided by the Spirit, Simeon could foresee the
influence of that babe's life and even, to some extent, the
suffering that His mother would endure because of the

rejection of His people. But Simeon could not envisage the perfect character that would develop as this child "increased in wisdom and stature, and in favor with God and men" (Luke 2:52). He could not meditate on the teaching that would come from His mouth or understand the significance of the atoning sacrifice that He would make. Nor could he know the intimate relationship of being "in Him" that is possible for us.

Such intimate knowledge should be the goal of each us before we "see death." This was the goal of the apostle Paul.

> But what things were gain to me, these I have counted loss for Christ. Yet indeed I also count all things loss for the excellence of the knowledge of Christ Jesus my Lord, for whom I have suffered the loss of all things, and count them as rubbish, that I may gain Christ and be found in Him, not having my own righteousness, which is from the law, but that which is through faith in Christ, the righteousness which is from God by faith; that I may know Him and the power of His resurrection, and the fellowship of His sufferings, being conformed to His death, if, by any means, I may attain to the resurrection from the dead (Philippians 3:7-11).

Indeed, we dare not die until we have come to know Him as our Savior. All the promises of future life depend, not on holding Him in our arms, but on having Him in our hearts: "Christ in you, the hope of glory" (Colossians 1:27).

We would see Jesus, for the shadows lengthen
Across this little landscape of our life;;
We would see Jesus, our weak faith to strengthen
For the last weariness, the final strife.

We would see Jesus; other lights are paling,
Which for long years we have rejoiced to see;
The blessings of our pilgrimage are failing;
We would not mourn them, for we go to Thee.

We would see Jesus: this is all we're needing;
Strength, joy, and willingness come with the sight;
We would see Jesus, dying, risen, pleading;
Then welcome day, and farewell mortal night.

– Anna B. Warner

Simeon warned Mary of the sword that would pierce her soul
(Luke 2:35). She must have remembered these words again
and again as she saw Him "despised and rejected of men; a
man of sorrows and acquainted with grief" (Isaiah 53:3).
Simeon's words may well have helped to keep her from being
disillusioned, even by the cross. She had been warned.

Though not possessing Simeon's inspiration, older parents
can often help young parents to understand some of the
challenges they face in rearing children. It is easy for young
parents to feel that all is lost when a child does something
disappointing or suffers some setback such as all children
experience. The best of parents can become so disappointed

with themselves that they virtually throw up their hands and withdraw from their responsibilities. It is then that older parents may be most helpful. We must be careful not to come on too strong with criticism of young parents, but gentle advice is appropriate and usually appreciated if it is given in the right spirit.

Anna

Another person came on the scene as Simeon was holding the baby Jesus.

> Now there was one, Anna, a prophetess, the daughter of Phanuel, of the tribe of Asher. She was of a great age, and had lived with a husband seven years from her virginity; and this woman was a widow of about eighty-four years, who did not depart from the temple, but served God with fastings and prayers night and day. And coming in that instant she gave thanks to the Lord, and spoke of Him to all those who looked for redemption in Jerusalem (Luke 2:36-38).

The age of this woman is not certain. The original language makes it difficult to determine if her age was eighty-four years or if she had been a widow for eighty-four years after living with a husband for seven years, in which case she would have been one hundred or more. Her great age may have been one of the reasons she "did not depart from the temple." Or, she may have been one of a group of aged widows who had simple duties to perform in the temple.

Her activities, serving "God with fastings and prayers night and day," are similar to those of widows who were to be cared for by the church. Widows in Bible times did not have the benefits that are commonly available today. The church was instructed to support exemplary Christian widows who were at least sixty years of age and had no other source of support. Such a widow was to be one who "trusts in God and continues in supplications and prayers night and day" (1 Timothy 5:5). The activities of Anna and those supported widows are commendable occupations for any older woman, supported by the church or not.

Simeon and Anna

With no desire to diminish the honor due to Simeon, there is an interesting contrast between him and Anna.

When Simeon saw little Jesus, he was ready to die. When Anna saw him, she was ready to speak "of Him to all those who looked for redemption in Jerusalem" (Luke 2:37).

If angels and shepherds were the first to announce the arrival of the Savior to Bethlehem, Anna was the first to announce it to Jerusalem. Thirty-three years later, another woman, Mary Magdalene, was the first eye-witness to announce the resurrection of that same Savior (Mark 16:9).

Simeon, in some ways, symbolized the old law of Moses. It looked forward to the coming of the Messiah, but when He came the law was fulfilled and was taken away (Galatians

3:19, Colossians 2:14). Anna symbolized the new covenant as she "spoke of Him to all those who looked for redemption." .

> Woman in the person of Anna might well rejoice; for in the kingdom of Christ there is neither male nor female;" all distinction of sex is unknown. Woman is free to enter that kingdom as man; she may reach as high a position, by personal excellency, in it; she is welcome to render holy service and fruitful testimony; is as certain to reap the reward of fidelity in the kingdom of heaven to which it leads. Women were the most faithful attendants on our Lord during his earthly ministry; they have been, since then, the most regular worshippers and the most devoted workers in his church. (W. Clarkson in *Pulpit Commentary*, Vol. 16, p.55)

Roles in the kingdom differ but greatness is attained, not by appointment but by service (Matthew 20:20-28). Though women are clearly instructed to "keep silent in the churches" (1 Corinthians 14:34) and forbidden to "teach or to have authority over a man" (1 Timothy 2:12), they are in no way prohibited from serving as Anna and many Christian women have done since that day.

Titus was to instruct older women to be,

> teachers of good things— that they admonish the young women to love their husbands, to love their children, to be discreet, chaste, homemakers, good, obedient to their own husbands, that the word of God may not be blasphemed" (Titus 2:3-5).

Without doubt, Timothy's mother and grandmother were responsible for the fact "that from childhood [he had] known the Holy Scriptures" (2 Timothy 3:15).

The eloquent preacher, Apollos. came to the synagogue in Ephesus teaching "accurately the things of the Lord, though he knew only the baptism of John…When Aquila and Priscilla heard him, they took him aside and explained to him the way of God more accurately" (Acts 18:25-26). Priscilla was active with her husband in this noble undertaking.

In many a church, godly women have been among the most fruitful teachers of the word without violating any of the restrictions stated by the Holy Spirit. Very often, baptisms that are credited to an evangelist have been the result of the influence and teaching of Christian women. A class of seniors was asked to list the ways that they had observed women participating in the teaching of the gospel. They listed praying for gospel teachers, teaching by phone or by skype, writing letters of encouragement to evangelists, conducting bible correspondence courses, teaching women in their homes, teaching children, showing hospitality, using social media, inviting others to services—and then the time ran out.

The fruitfulness of many an evangelist has been made possible by a faithful, dedicated wife. Without doubt, whatever their husbands accomplish is to their account (Philippians 4:17).

O God, You have taught me from my youth;
And to this day I declare Your wondrous works.

Now also when I am old and grayheaded,
O God, do not forsake me,
Until I declare Your strength to this generation,
Your power to everyone who is to come.
Psalm 71:17-18

Burny and Barbara Leavitt

Like Simeon, Burny Leavitt desired to see "the Lord's Christ." Burny, too, had a promise: "Blessed are those who hunger and thirst for righteousness, for they shall be filled" (Matthew 5:6). And in the Lord's providence, he came to know the Lord when he was 34 years old.

Burny desired to preach the gospel and entered Florida College where he met his future wife, Barbara, who was fifteen years his junior. Like Anna, Barbara, too, was eager to share the gospel and the sixty years of their lives together have been spent in a variety of needy places, speaking of the Christ to all who will listen.

Soon after their marriage they found their way back to Vermont, Burny's native state, where they started a church in their home. When this effort proved fruitless, after a brief stay in Abilene, TX, they were on their way to spend four years preaching in Belize. Some time after returning to the States, they bought a travel trailer, a suburban to pull it, and a motorcycle for transportation and hit the road. Wherever there was a small struggling church in Georgia, Kentucky or North or South Carolina, one would not be surprised to find the Leavitts.

Later they moved to North Florida to help for nine months
in the prison work that had been started a number of years
earlier by Daryl Townsend. Then after three more years in
North Georgia, working again with small congregations,
Burny was ninety-one. But this did not prevent their going
back to the prison work for three more years.

Greg Whipple, who worked with Daryl Townsend and the
Leavitts reports:

> They had a real love for the men, especially those at the
> transition house. They would often go to the studies there.
> ... Their continued work into a time when most have
> felt comfortable taking a well-deserved rest is a personal
> encouragement to me. Burny taught in seven prisons,
> sometimes with as many as forty Christians in attendance
> for Sunday services. Barbara visited two women's prisons.

According to Barbara Leavitt, while Burny was teaching and
preaching, she sent Bible correspondence course lessons to
inmates.

Meanwhile, they had sold their log home in the North
Georgia mountains and, living again in a travel trailer,
they used the proceeds from the sale to assist financially
where there was a need. When Burny's health and hearing
deteriorated to the point that they could no longer serve, he
preached his last sermon in prison at the age of 94 and they
returned to Georgia to live in the finished basement of their
daughter.

Even today, aged men and women can serve in the church of the Lord as Simeon and Anna served in the Temple.

> The righteous shall flourish like a palm tree,
> He shall grow like a cedar in Lebanon.
> Those who are planted in the house of the Lord
> Shall flourish in the courts of our God.
> They shall still bear fruit in old age;
> They shall be fresh and flourishing,
> To declare that the Lord is upright;
> He is my rock, and there is no unrighteousness in Him.
> (Psalm 92:12-15)

Memory Work

Fill in the blanks from memory: Therefore we do not lose ___ ___. Even though our _____ man is _____, yet the _____ man is being _____ day by day. For our _ _____ _____, which is but for a _____, is working for us a far more _____ and _____ _____ __ of _____, while we do not _____ at the things which are _____, but at the things which are not _____. For the things which are seen are _____, but the things which are not seen are _____ (2 Corinthians 4:16-18).

Questions

1. Do you have something specific in your mind that you want to do before you die?

2. What promise had been made to Simeon?

3. When was this promise fulfilled?

4. What three things did Simeon say about the baby (Luke 2:30-32)?

5. Why do you think Joseph and Mary marveled at these things?

6. Meaningful as it would be to hold the baby Jesus in our arms, what greater blessings do we enjoy in reference to Jesus?

7. What warning did Simeon give Mary? Can you think of any value this might have been to her as the life of Jesus progressed?

8. How old was Anna?

9. What was Anna doing in the temple?

10. What were the qualifications necessary for a woman in the early church to be enrolled and supported to do much the same (1 Timothy 5:3-16)?

11. What did Anna begin to do after she had seen Jesus? What distinction did this give her? Did she violate the restrictions on women's roles contained in 1 Corinthians 14:34 and 1 Timothy 2:9-10?

12. Do those restrictions limit their opportunity for greatness (Matthew 20:25-28)?

13. What teaching does Titus 2:3-5 specifically authorize older women to do?

14. What are some other things that older women can do in the Lord's service?

15. Do you know of women who render significant service in the church?

Chapter 12

Paul

"Paul, the aged" (Philemon 1:1)

In any list of Senior complaints, the following will almost inevitably appear:

- Pain

- Loneliness

- Regrets for the past

- Anxiety facing death

- Concern for those left behind.

In his letter to Philemon, Paul refers to himself as "Paul, the aged." He may not have been much over sixty, but that was older in his day than it is now. In addition, he had undergone the kind of hardships that age the body prematurely. We are greatly blessed by his writings that reveal how he dealt with all the realities listed above.

How Paul Dealt with Pain

In Second Corinthians 12:7-10, Paul speaks of his "thorn in the flesh." Some translations call it a "stake in the flesh." If a thorn is painful, as most of us can testify, think how a stake would feel. No one knows for sure what his thorn was but, knowing Paul's zeal for preaching, it seems likely that he considered this thorn not only painful, but a hindrance to his work. How did he handle it?

> And lest I should be exalted above measure by the abundance of the revelations, a thorn in the flesh was given to me, a messenger of Satan to buffet me, lest I be exalted above measure. Concerning this thing I pleaded with the Lord three times that it might depart from me. And He said to me, "My grace is sufficient for you, for My strength is made perfect in weakness." Therefore most gladly I will rather boast in my infirmities, that the power of Christ may rest upon me. Therefore I take pleasure in infirmities, in reproaches, in needs, in persecutions, in distresses, for Christ's sake. For when I am weak, then I am strong.

Several facts stand out. First, he blamed Satan and not God. At the same time, he believed enough in God's power to remove it that he prayed three times for its removal. These must have been prayers like the prayer of Daniel when special times were set aside to petition God. When God did not remove it, he sought for some good that might come from it; twice he noted that it kept him humble even when he could have been proud. That being so, he would not only endure it, but even rejoice in it as well as in other experiences that God might allow him to suffer.

When we suffer pain, what is our first reaction? Surely it is not wrong to reach for the aspirin or the acetaminophen to obtain some relief. Neither is it wrong to seek the advice of a physician. But how long do we have to suffer and how excruciating does the pain have to become before we set aside a time to pray fervently to God for relief? Do we really believe that God hears prayers and that he is able and willing to respond when it is for our good?

If the pain remains, we should remember that pain can be a blessing. Pain is a reminder of our mortality, something all of us need regardless of age. Pain can increase our influence for good when, in spite of it, we persist in working for the Lord. An aged sister in our home congregation is in obvious pain as she faithfully comes to services, pushing the wheel chair of her grandson. Yet, there she is, week after week and service after service. Without entering the pulpit, she preaches a sermon on faithfulness that is more eloquent than most preachers could possibly deliver.

We do not seek pain, but neither do we let it destroy our happiness or prevent our faithfulness.

How Paul Dealt with Loneliness

It is easy for us to imagine that Paul was almost superhuman. A study of his activities as reported by Luke, the physician, as well as things he wrote in his epistles remind us of his humanity.

Paul obviously did not like to be alone. He was usually with
fellow-workers, those his age as well as younger men. Once,
when threats to his life forced him to leave Berea and travel
to Athens alone, he left a "command for Silas and Timothy
to come to him with all speed" (Acts 17:15). Timothy joined
him, but Paul's anxiety for the persecuted Thessalonians
moved him "to be left in Athens alone, and [to send]
Timothy…to establish you and encourage you concerning
your faith" (1 Thessalonians 3:1-2).

How did he use his loneliness in Athens? He did not use it
for sight-seeing or "resting up." Rather "he reasoned in the
synagogue with the Jews and with the Gentile worshipers,
and in the marketplace daily with those who happened to
be there" (Acts 17:17). He did not let loneliness prevent his
working for the Lord.

During his last imprisonment he was grieved when many
old friends forsook him. He reported, "All those in Asia
have turned away from me, among whom are Phygellus and
Hermogenes" (2 Timothy 1:15). Demas forsook him, "having
loved this present world" (2 Timothy 4:8). Others had left for
various places, hopefully for kingdom duties. Only Luke was
with him and he urged Timothy: "Do your utmost to come
before winter" (2 Timothy 4:21).

One of the saddest pictures in all the Bible is the scene Paul
describes in Second Timothy 4:16. "At my first defense no
one stood with me, but all forsook me. May it not be charged
against them." And how did he deal with that? The next

verse provides the answer. "But the Lord stood with me and strengthened me." Faith in the presence of the Lord is the very best antidote to loneliness.

How Paul Dealt with Regrets from his Past

If any Christian has ever had reason to regret events in his past, it was Paul. No report of his sinful conduct is more graphic than his own account offered on more than one occasion.

> Many of the saints I shut up in prison, having received authority from the chief priests; and when they were put to death, I cast my vote against them. And I punished them often in every synagogue and compelled them to blaspheme; and being exceedingly enraged against them, I persecuted them even to foreign cities" (Acts 26:10-11).

He identified himself as the chief of sinners (1 Timothy 1:15).

How did Paul deal with those memories?

He did not forget his past, but neither did he let it intimidate him to the point of destroying his effectiveness. He still could say, "I consider that I am not at all inferior to the most eminent apostles" (2 Corinthians 11:5).

He let his future goals supersede his memory of past mistakes.

> Brethren, I do not count myself to have apprehended; but one thing I do, forgetting those things which are behind

and reaching forward to those things which are ahead, I press toward the goal for the prize of the upward call of God in Christ Jesus" (Philippians 3:13-14).

Furthermore, any sense of guilt that remained was offset by his faith in the grace and forgiveness of God. In the very context in which he designates himself the chief of sinners he explains the reason for his acceptance in the ministry. "And the grace of our Lord was exceedingly abundant, with faith and love which are in Christ Jesus" (1 Timothy 1:14). A remaining sense of guilt, once we are in Christ, is not a becoming humility but a regrettable lack of faith in the grace of God. The scriptures are clear. "There is therefore now no condemnation to those who are in Christ Jesus" (Romans 8:1). "In Him we have redemption through His blood, the forgiveness of sins, according to the riches of His grace" (Ephesians 1:7).

How Paul Faced Death

Fear of death is natural in those who are aging. The Bible speaks of "those who through fear of death were all their lifetime subject to bondage" (Hebrews 2:15). King Saul's fear of death led him to seek a witch to provide some vision of his fate (1 Samuel 28:5-20). Isaiah 38:10-13 is a lament of good King Hezekiah as he anticipated his death.

Paul faced death again and again in his lifetime as he was beaten, stoned, and shipwrecked. Never did he express the slightest fear.

Once before a Roman court, he said, "If I am an offender, or have committed anything deserving of death, I do not object to dying" (Acts 25:11). To the Philippians he wrote,

> To me, to live is Christ, and to die is gain. But if I live on in the flesh, this will mean fruit from my labor; yet what I shall choose I cannot tell. For I am hard-pressed between the two, having a desire to depart and be with Christ, which is far better" (Philippians 1:21-23).

Death to Paul meant exchanging this earthly tent for a heavenly mansion. "For we know that if our earthly house, this tent, is destroyed, we have a building from God, a house not made with hands, eternal in the heavens" (2 Corinthians 5:1).

Some people talk glowingly of death until they know they are facing it. When Paul wrote Second Timothy, he knew that death was imminent. This made no difference; he still faced it with confidence:

> I have fought the good fight, I have finished the race, I have kept the faith. Finally, there is laid up for me the crown of righteousness, which the Lord, the righteous Judge, will give to me on that Day, and not to me only but also to all who have loved His appearing" (2 Timothy 4:6-8).

Faith may not keep us from dreading death. Jesus dreaded it. But anticipation of future glory can make it bearable. The dread of the journey is diminished by anticipation of the destination.

The sands of time are sinking,,
The dawn of heaven breaks;
The summer morn I've sighed for –
The fair, sweet morn awakes:
Dark, dark had been the midnight
But Dayspring is at hand,
And glory, glory dwelleth
In Emmanuel's land.

The king there in His beauty,
Without a veil is seen:
It were a well-spent journey,
Though seven deaths lay between:
The Lamb with His fair army,
Doth on Mount Zion stand,
And glory, glory dwelleth
In Emmanuel's land.   — Ann Cousin

How Paul Dealt With Concern for Those Left Behind

Paul listed among his many sufferings "my deep concern for all the churches." Then he added, "Who is weak, and I am not weak? Who is made to stumble, and I do not burn with indignation?" (2 Corinthians 11:28-29).

It would be inevitable that Paul's concern for his brethren would reach beyond his life on earth. His concerns, however, were not so much for their physical or material well-being, but for their faithfulness. When he expected that the Ephesian elders would never see him again, he warned them:

> Therefore take heed to yourselves and to all the flock, among which the Holy Spirit has made you overseers, to shepherd the church of God which He purchased with His own blood. For I know this, that after my departure savage wolves will come in among you, not sparing the flock. Also from among yourselves men will rise up, speaking perverse things, to draw away the disciples after themselves. Therefore watch, and remember that for three years I did not cease to warn everyone night and day with tears (Acts 20:28-31).

His last epistle, Second Timothy, was almost entirely an appeal to Timothy to be strong and faithful. His concern, even for generations to follow, was expressed also. "And the things that you have heard from me among many witnesses, commit these to faithful men who will be able to teach others also" (2 Timothy 2:2).

Paul prayed for those who would be left behind, he warned and admonished those to whom he had access, and he wrote letters to others.

Most of us find ourselves burdened by concern for our children and grandchildren when we are gone. We worry about the possibility of future wars they may have to endure, about oppressive governments under which they may live, about economic hardships they may have to bear, and other imponderable sufferings they may experience. But none of these can compare to the spiritual dangers they face now and will face.

Paul's example should instruct us. Pray for them. Admonish them while we live. And write letters to them which may have more meaning to them after we are gone than when they receive them.

Dying words are especially impressive to those who are left behind. My brother and I have a letter addressed to us by our father near the end of his life, and it has been a source of encouragement to us as we have read it again and again. This is something parents can do even as the sun of life is setting.

> Even to *your* old age, I *am* He,
> And *even* to gray hairs I will carry *you*!
> I have made, and I will bear;
> Even I will carry, and will deliver *you* (Isaiah 46:4).

Memory Work

Fill in the blanks from memory:

> Therefore we do not lose _____. Even though our
> _____ man is _____, yet the _____ man
> is being _____ day by day. For our _____ ___
> _____, which is but for a _____, is working for us a
> far more _____ and _____ _____ of

_____, while we do not _____ at the things which
are _____, but at the things which are not _____. For
the _____ _____ __ _____ are _____, but the
things _____ ____ _____ _____are _____
__ (2 Corinthians 4:16-18).

Questions

1. What does Paul call the pain that he suffered? Who did he blame for it?

2. What does he report that he did to find relief?

3. What does this indicate about his faith in God's power?

4. How did he react when the pain was not taken away?

5. What are some indications that Paul did not like to be alone?

6. Who are some who abandoned him during his last imprisonment?

7. Where did he find comfort when he was left alone to face his first defense? What lesson can we gain from this?

8. Name some individuals who were fearful because of the sins of their earlier life?

9. What past sins did Paul have to regret?

10. Why do you think he showed no sense of guilt in his later years? If we as Christians continue to feel guilty about sins of our youth, what does this indicate?

11. Who are some individuals in the Bible who dreaded death?

12. In Paul's earlier years, what sentiments did he express regarding death?

13. Did the reality of imminent death change his perspective?

14. Why do you think he was so willing to die?

15. Is death a curse or a blessing for those who die "in the Lord" (Revelation 14:13)?

16. What are some concerns most of us have for the future of our children and grandchildren?

17. What is the most serious danger they face?

18. As Paul faced death, what did he do out of concern for Timothy?

19. What did Paul charge Timothy to do that would affect future generations?

20. Does this suggest some things we may do out of concern for those we will leave behind?

Chapter 13

$\mathcal{H}ope$

*"In hope of eternal life which God, who cannot lie,
promised before time began" (Titus 1:2).*

Young people know that death will come eventually, but they are quite sure it will not be soon. Those of us who are aging realize that it is fast approaching. With every new twinge of pain or awareness of weakness we wonder, "Could this be it?" This awareness can be a source of terror or of calm anticipation, or of something in between. So much depends on faith.

Gerontologist David L. Petty writes,

> "I think it is essential to recognize the fact that as we are growing older, we also are dying—physically, of course; hopefully, not spiritually. ... Death is God-ordained; indeed, He gives us ample indications of this fact in his written word (c.f. 2 Kings 14:6; Ecclesiastes 3:2; Hebrews 9:27; and Romans 6:23). Death, like aging, is both

inevitable and irresistible. Dealing with death and dying is healthy; denying or suppressing these realities is unhealthy. In fact, denial creates the worst kind of "giant of despair" in our lives. While facing death head-on with courage may not be easy, it is possible" (Psalm 23:4). – *Aging Gracefully* p. 122

Those without God are without hope (Ephesians 2:12)—at least, without a valid hope. They may be optimistic and have a warm feeling about the future, but they have no solid evidence on which to base it. The noted atheist, Robert Ingersoll, expressed such an unfounded hope when speaking at his brother's grave.

Life is a narrow vale between the cold and barren peaks of two eternities. We strive in vain to look beyond the heights. We cry aloud, and the only answer is the echo of our wailing cry. From the voiceless lips of the un-replying dead there comes no word; but in the night of death hope sees a star, and listening love can hear the rustle of a wing.

Christians, on the other hand, "sorrow not as others who have no hope" (1 Thessalonians 4:13). Their hope is firmly based. It is firmly rooted in "the Lord Jesus Christ, our hope" (1 Timothy 1:1).

2 Corinthians 4:16—5:10

From the very beginning of this study we have encouraged memorizing Second Corinthians 4:16-18. We called it the

golden text for the golden aged. It deserves an even closer
look in this last chapter.

> Therefore we do not lose heart. Even though our outward
> man is perishing, yet the inward man is being renewed day
> by day. For our light affliction, which is but for a moment,
> is working for us a far more exceeding and eternal weight
> of glory, while we do not look at the things which are seen,
> but at the things which are not seen. For the things which
> are seen are temporary, but the things which are not seen
> are eternal.

As noted earlier, Paul dealt with the decaying condition of his
outward man by concentrating on his inward man.

The afflictions he suffered in his outward man were more
stressful than most of us have ever known. He lists some of
them for us:

> In stripes above measure, in prisons more frequently, in
> deaths often. From the Jews five times I received forty
> stripes minus one. Three times I was beaten with rods;
> once I was stoned; three times I was shipwrecked; a night
> and a day I have been in the deep; in journeys often, in
> perils of waters, in perils of robbers, in perils of my own
> countrymen, in perils of the Gentiles, in perils in the city,
> in perils in the wilderness, in perils in the sea, in perils
> among false brethren; in weariness and toil, in sleeplessness
> often, in hunger and thirst, in fastings often, in cold and
> nakedness (2 Corinthians 11:23-27).

Earlier in 2 Corinthians 4, he reveals that he did not let such afflictions defeat him. "We are hard-pressed on every side, yet not crushed; we are perplexed, but not in despair; persecuted, but not forsaken; struck down, but not destroyed" (verses 8.9). How could he endure these hardships?

Paul discounted the "afflictions" of the outward man by comparing them with the "glory" awaiting the inward man. He counted them "light" compared with the "exceeding weight" of the glory he anticipated. And, though he had suffered those afflictions for most of forty years, they were "but for a moment" compared to the "eternal glory" that he fully expected (verses 16-18). Faith is the remedy for fear.

The comparisons of the seen and the unseen in the fourth chapter are continued in chapter five. Paul speaks of our physical body as a tent compared to our future home, a "building from God, a house not made with hands, eternal in the heavens" (verse 1). Who would not be glad to move from a tent to a house, especially one built by God? In death, our mortality with which we have struggled is "swallowed up by life" (verse 4). And departure from the body means "to be present with the Lord" (verse 8).

> When all my labors and trials are o'er,
> And I am safe on that beautiful shore,
> Just to be near the dear Lord I adore
> Will through the ages be glory for me.
> Charles H. Gabriel

If we can just learn as Paul to "walk by faith, and not by sight" (verse 7) we can come to terms with the prospect of death. We may dread the journey, but eagerly anticipate the destination.

"Jesus Christ, Our Hope"

1 Timothy 1:1

His Promises give us hope in death:

> Do not marvel at this; for the hour is coming in which all who are in the graves will hear His voice and come forth—those who have done good, to the resurrection of life, and those who have done evil, to the resurrection of condemnation (John 5:28-29).

Speaking to Martha, whose brother Lazarus had died, Jesus said to her,

> I am the resurrection and the life. He who believes in Me, though he may die, he shall live. And whoever lives and believes in Me shall never die. Do you believe this? (John 11:25-26).

His Works prove his ability to fulfill his promises. Otherwise, the promises would be empty words. Immediately after these reassuring words to Martha, He went with her and her sister to the tomb where Lazarus was dead.

"Then Jesus, again groaning in Himself, came to the tomb. It was a cave, and a stone lay against it" (John 11:38).

> When Jesus stood at Lazarus' tomb
> And none believed he had the power,
> Despite their grief, and their disbelief,
> He commanded, "Take away the stone."
> — Robert L. Morrison and Gary L. Box

He cried with a loud voice, "Lazarus, come forth!" And he who had died came out bound hand and foot with graveclothes, and his face was wrapped with a cloth. Jesus said to them, "Loose him, and let him go" (John 11:43-44).

His cross makes possible the "resurrection of life" for those who have done good. Good deeds alone cannot atone for the sins of which we all are guilty. Anticipating His death on a cross He predicted:

> As Moses lifted up the serpent in the wilderness, even so must the Son of Man be lifted up, that whoever believes in Him should not perish but have eternal life. (John 3:14-15)

> But God demonstrates His own love toward us, in that while we were still sinners, Christ died for us. (Romans 5:8)

His Resurrection validates His death for our sins and assures the resurrection of "those who are Christ's at His coming."

> When Jesus lay in Joseph's tomb,
> And none believed he had the power,
> True love spoke forth in a Father's voice
> And the angel took away the stone.
> — Robert L. Morrison and Gary L. Box

> But now Christ is risen from the dead, and has become the firstfruits of those who have fallen asleep. For since by man came death, by Man also came the resurrection of the dead. For as in Adam all die, even so in Christ all shall be made alive. But each one in his own order: Christ the firstfruits, afterward those who are Christ's at His coming. (1 Corinthians 15:20-23).

> For if we believe that Jesus died and rose again, even so God will bring with Him those who sleep in Jesus. (1 Thessalonians 4:14)

His Ascension took Him to the throne of God. He entered heaven, the true Holy Place, just as the High Priest for centuries had entered annually into the typical holy place in the tabernacle. There He made atonement for our sins, and there He makes intercession for us. His ministry there is our hope for the future.

> This hope we have as an anchor of the soul, both sure and steadfast, and which enters the Presence behind the veil,

where the forerunner has entered for us, even Jesus, having become High Priest forever according to the order of Melchizedek (Hebrews 6:19-20).

Normally an anchor goes down to stabilize a ship. Our anchor is on high, taken there by our high priest who ascended to minister until His future return.

His Return is as certain as his ascension. When He ascended, two angels appeared and said to those who were observing,

> Men of Galilee, why do you stand gazing up into heaven? This same Jesus, who was taken up from you into heaven, will so come in like manner as you saw Him go into heaven (Acts 1:11)

> The Lord Himself will descend from heaven with a shout, with the voice of an archangel, and with the trumpet of God. And the dead in Christ will rise first. Then we who are alive and remain shall be caught up together with them in the clouds to meet the Lord in the air. And thus we shall always be with the Lord (1 Thessalonians 4:16-17).

> When I shall lie within my tomb,
> And none believe he has the pwoer,
> The Lord Himself will descend from heaven
> With a shout, to take away the stone.
> — Robert L. Morrison and Gary L. Box

Do You Believe This?

When Jesus promised Martha that not only her brother, but all who believe in Him would live again, he asked, "Do you believe this?" (John 11:25). This is the question we all should ask of ourselves: "Do I believe this?"

The student in college can live with boring classes, term papers and challenging exams because he anticipates his graduation and the opportunities his education will provide. The runner can endure the pain and weariness of the race because he hopes for the medal at the finish line. The farmer can labor from dawn till dusk in the field as he foresees the harvest in the fall. The soldier can brave the dangers of the battle field as he dreams of going home. Such anticipation inspires the Christian.

> When the last feeble step has been taken,
> And the gates of that city appear,
> When the beautiful songs of the angels
> Float out on my listening ear;
> When all that now seem so mysterious
> Will be bright and as clear as the day;
> Then the toils of the road will seem nothing
> When I get to the end of the way.
> — Charles D. Tillman

Memory Work

Fill in the blanks from memory:

Therefore we do not lose _____. Even though our
_____ man is _____, yet the _____ man
is being _____ day by day. For our _____ ____
_____, which is but for a _____, is _____ ___ ___
a far more _____ and _____ _____
of _____, while we do not _____ at the things which
are _____, but at the things _____ ____ not _____.
For the _____ _____ ___ _____ are _____,
but the things _____ ____ _____ _____are _____
_____ (2 Corinthians 4:16-18).

Questions

1. What makes death more real to those who are older?

2. What are some things about approaching death that we dread?

3. What gives a Christian reason not to sorrow as others?

4. From the 2 Corinthians 4:16-18, what does Paul compare with:

Affliction?

Light?

For a moment?

Things that are seen

Temporary

5. Why is our earthly body called a tent?

6. What will replace it?

7. According to 2 Corinthians 5:7, what makes the thought of dying tolerable for Christians?

8. What are some promises of Jesus that give us hope?

9. How did He prove His power to raise the dead?

10. How does faith in the cross give Christians comfort in death?

11. What is His resurrection called in 1 Corinthians 15:20

and 23?

12. When Jesus ascended into heaven, what did He take with Him (Hebrews 6:20)

13. What was promised when He ascended into heaven (Acts 1:8-11)?

14. What will happen to those who are dead in Christ when He comes (1 Thessalonians 4:17)?

15. From 1 Corinthians 15:42-44, what change will take place in the body that was buried?

> It was buried corruptible It will be raised _____
>
> It was buried in dishonor It will be raised _____
>
> It was buried in weakness It will be raised _____
>
> It was buried a physical body   It will be raised _____

16. What is the precious promise of 1 John 3:2?

> For our citizenship is in heaven, from which we also eagerly wait for the Savior, the Lord Jesus Christ, who will transform our lowly body that it may be conformed to His glorious body, according to the working by which He is able even to subdue all things to Himself (Philippians 3:20-21).

"If Winter comes, can Spring be far behind?"

Percy Bysshe Shelly

Works Cited

Apter, Terri *What Do You Want From Me?* New York-London: W.W. Norton & Company, 2008

Barclay, William *The Letters to Timothy, Titus and Philemon.* The New Daily Study Bible, Louisville, KY: Westminster John Knox Press, 1975

Bowman, Dee *The Joy of Growing Old in Christ.* Lakeland, FL: Harwell/Lewis Publishing, 2019

Buchanan, Missy *Talking with God in Old Age.* Nashville, TN: Upper Room: 2010

Chapman, C. *First and Second Samuel.* The Pulpit Commentary. Grand Rapids, MI: Wm. B. Eerdmans, 1950

Clarkson, W. Luke. *The Pulpit Comentary, Grand Rapids, MI:* Wm. B. Eerdmans Publishing Company, 1950.

Godwin, Johnnie *How to Retire Without Retreating.* Uhrichsville, OH: Barbour Publishing, 2000

Norris, Bill and Judy *What the Bible Says About Growing Old.* Joplin, MO: College Press, 1988

Petty, David L. *Aging Gracefully.* Nashville, TN: Broadman and Holman, 2003

Rimmer, Harry *The Prayer Perfect*. New York, NY: Fleming H. Revell, 1940

Spence, H. D. M. *Genesis. The Pulpit Commentary*. Grand Rapids, MI: Wm. B. Eerdmans Publishing Company, 1950

Spence, H. D. M. *Ruth*. Grand Rapids, MI: Wm. B. Eerdmans Publishing Company, 1950

Made in the USA
Columbia, SC
15 February 2020